City Bias and Rural Neglect: The Dilemma of Urban Development

The Population Council

Michael P. Todaro
with Jerry Stilkin

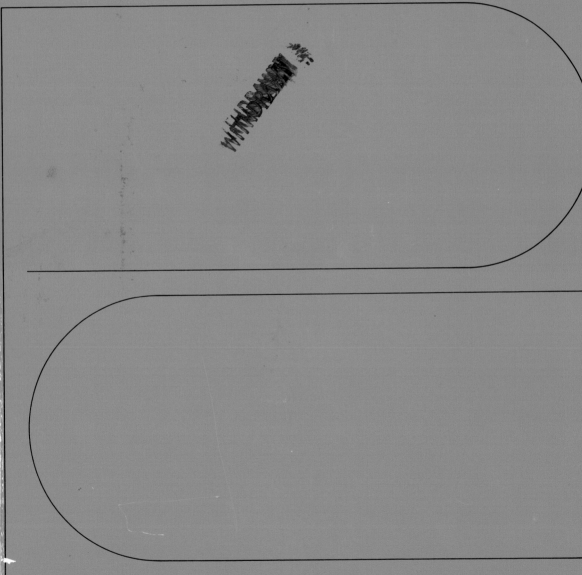

The Population Council is an independent, nonprofit organization established in 1952 at the initiative of John D. Rockefeller 3rd. It is international in the composition of its Board of Trustees and its staff, as well as in the nature and deployment of its activities. The Council conducts multidisciplinary research and provides technical and professional services in the broad field of population. Its various activities reflect eight primary program themes: interaction between population and development processes, policies, and programs; demographic aspects of family and community behavior; migration and urbanization; women in development; contraceptive development; physiology of the reproductive system of the human male; approaches to birth planning; and monitoring the safety and health effects of methods of fertility regulation. In addition to these eight themes, strengthening professional resources is an important element that runs through the Council's programs. The Council maintains collaborative relationships with institutions throughout the world having similar interests. It awards grants and contracts both to extend and complement its own work and to help build, enlarge, or strengthen professional resources elsewhere. In addition, the Council awards training opportunities and fellowships of several kinds intended to increase the number of qualified professionals in the population field. The Council disseminates publications and information on population matters to interested individuals and groups.

Public Issues papers of the Population Council are a hybrid form of policy writing: part *descriptive* of current knowledge; part *analytical* in suggesting alternative interpretations of this knowledge; part *policy directed* in weighing possible responses and in suggesting directions for future action. Public Issues papers relate insights gained from Council staff research to issues of contemporary policy relevance, in the United States and elsewhere, and present arguments in a condensed, nontechnical format. Papers in this series do not necessarily reflect the views of the Population Council.

Papers in the Public Issues series:

Toward Safe, Convenient, and Effective Contraceptives: A Policy Perspective
Stephen L. Salyer and James J. Bausch

U.S. Immigration: A Policy Analysis
Charles B. Keely

Contraceptives and Common Sense: Conventional Methods Reconsidered
Judith Bruce and S. Bruce Schearer

City Bias and Rural Neglect: The Dilemma of Urban Development
Michael P. Todaro, with Jerry Stilkind

Public Issues activities and papers are supported, in part, by a grant from the George Gund Foundation.

City Bias
and Rural Neglect:
The Dilemma
of Urban Development

City Bias
and Rural Neglect:
The Dilemma
of Urban Development

a Public Issues paper of
The Population Council

Michael P. Todaro
with Jerry Stilkind

The Population Council
One Dag Hammarskjold Plaza
New York, N.Y. 10017 U.S.A.

Library of Congress Cataloging in Publication Data

Todaro, Michael P
 City bias and rural neglect.

 (A Public issues paper of the Population Council ; PI-04)
 Bibliography: p.
 1. Underdeveloped areas—Urbanization. 2. Underdeveloped areas
—Rural-urban migration. 3. Urban economics. 4. Urban policy.
I. Stilkind, Jerry, joint author. II. Title. III. Series: Population Coun-
cil, New York. Public issues paper of the Population Council ; PI-04.
HN980.T63   307.7'6   80–26071
ISBN 0–87834–042–4

Contents

This Public Issues paper attempts to deal in broad strokes with a critical but highly complex problem facing many contemporary developing nations— the rapid population growth of their major cities. Although it would be both desirable and convenient to be able to analyze urban population and development problems in isolation from the wider issues of alternative economic development strategies, this unfortunately is neither possible nor appropriate. Urbanization problems and policy options must be viewed in the context of wider social, economic, and demographic considerations. I have tried, therefore, to analyze these issues and to suggest appropriate government policy responses within the broad sweep of general development strategies, rather than focus solely on traditional issues more narrowly examined by urban scholars. This more general approach in combination with the "interested layman" orientation of Public Issues papers has necessitated that I focus on the "big questions" of urbanization as I perceive them. An obvious drawback of such a sweeping approach is the need occasionally to simplify more complex issues, to treat developing-world cities as if they were mostly the same, and, in general, to ignore some of the considerable complexities of urbanization problems as they are manifested in diverse developing nations. I am confident, however, that the benefits of this broad approach will clearly outweigh the costs of necessary simplifications.

Numerous people have been of great assistance to me in this endeavor. Foremost among them is Jerry Stilkind, who very ably assisted me by collecting and organizing a great quantity of research material, pulling it together according to an agreed-upon outline, and preparing early drafts of the paper. Patricia Beyea persuaded me of the importance of a Public Issues paper on this subject and provided considerable support and encouragement. Very helpful comments on earlier drafts were provided by James Bausch, Ethel Churchill, Arch Dotson, and Michael Mertaugh. Finally, Robert Heidel rendered invaluable copyediting services while Barbara Jackson and Kate Venet patiently typed and retyped successive drafts.

MICHAEL P. TODARO

The cities of the developing world are growing at an extremely rapid pace and many are becoming unmanageable. Millions of people in Africa, Asia, and Latin America pour in each year from the impoverished countrysides, swelling the ranks of the unemployed and straining the already limited supply of urban social services. These migration waves often result from government policies and private sector activities that are making the rural areas poorer than ever and the cities so large that shanty towns and crime are rapidly increasing.

In 1950, only four of the world's 15 largest cities were located in developing countries. By the year 2000, 12 will be. Mexico City is expected to be the largest with a population exceeding 30 million. During the last quarter of this century, the number of developing-world cities with populations exceeding 4 million is expected to almost quadruple, from 16 to 61 localities.

The rapid urbanization of much of the developing world is not simply part of the birth pangs of an industrialization that eventually will grow strong enough to provide adequately for almost all of the people—as happened in the Western countries. Rather, it is an outgrowth of a philosophy and a failed strategy of development that has emphasized industrial and urban growth at the expense of agriculture and rural development.

Problems of rapid urbanization can only be overcome by policies that are more evenly balanced between the needs of the cities and the requirements of the countryside. If urban economic, social, and educational preferences are not reduced, rural areas will never be able to develop fully and the major cities will continue to grow rapidly.

In regions where it is not possible to stimulate both the industrial urban and the rural sectors, the time has come to give relatively less to the cities. Unless there are much greater investments in agriculture and rural nonfarm enterprises, developing countries will be unable to solve their pressing urban problems. If the countryside does not prosper, the migrant flow will continue and the cities will deteriorate. This is the paradox of the urban dilemma in developing countries: to help the cities, development must be focused on the rural areas.

Past policies that emphasized urban industrial growth at the expense of agriculture and rural development often produced economies hopelessly unbalanced between a small but growing manufacturing sector and a vast but stagnating, or barely growing agricultural sector. They helped to create an agriculture so unproductive that per capita food output declined in 56 developing countries during the 1960s and in 13 more the following decade. They helped to create an urban growth so rapid that the proportion of developing-world populations living in cities jumped from 16.7 percent in 1950 to 25.8 percent in 1970, with a figure of 43.5 percent expected by the end of the century. Urban industry simply cannot absorb these numbers.

The strategy of rapid industrialization dominated economic development thinking and practice from the end of World War II until the 1970s and, in many countries, continues to dominate to this day. By the mid-1970s, however, the failures in agriculture had become so conspicuous that an alternative policy evolved—rural development. Unfortunately, where a program to stimulate agriculture was adopted, it often was done on top of, not instead of, the tax breaks, tariff protection, and subsidized interest rates being granted to heavy industry. Along with creating some improvements in the countryside, governments continued to build better roads, schools, water works, and electric generating stations in the capital and other large cities.

These government-supplied services were a major inducement to industry to locate in the principal cities. Urban wages in both the private and the public sector were substantially higher than in any other part of the country. Furthermore, unions in many cities effectively organized industrial workers while governments protected them with steadily rising minimum wages. The ultimate result of these policies was to create incomes and services in the cities far superior to those in rural areas, leading millions to migrate in search of a better livelihood. Rural-to-urban migration has become so overwhelming in some countries that a degrading life of slum-centered poverty is the likely fate of both new migrants and urban natives.

Most developing countries have lately become concerned about the degree of overurbanization they are experiencing. A 1977 United Nations survey found that 113 out of 119 developing-country governments considered the geographic distribution of their population unacceptable. Some 94 countries on all continents reported they had adopted policies to affect the distribution of their peoples, ranging from trying to slow or even reverse migration to cities to lowering fertility rates.

But this government concern over excessive urbanization has not attracted sufficient attention among economists and other social scientists, thus depriving political leaders and administrators of a reasoned analysis and deeper understanding of the problem and possible solutions. One reason for the lack of attention may be that such a phenomenon was never anticipated. Overurbanization did not occur in the economic growth of the West because, broadly speaking, migrants were absorbed by industry in the cities or they moved to new territories overseas. They were a source of cheap labor to infant industries 100 years ago, and, assuming the continued availability of jobs, it was thought that migrants today could perform the same function in the developing countries. Another reason for this lack of attention may be that it is not yet possible to measure overurbanization, neither the point at which it begins nor its magnitude.

But developing countries are in a far different position today from the developed countries on the eve of their industrialization. The major difference is that there are many more people today attempting to enter industries that require much less labor.

If overurbanization cannot be measured to the statistical satisfaction of social scientists, it certainly can be recognized. There are at least three signs indicating its presence: (1) the number of unemployed and underemployed in the cities is large and growing; (2) the proportion of the urban labor force working in industry is scarcely growing and may be declining in some countries; (3) the sheer numbers of people in the cities and the rapidity of population growth are so great that few countries can adequately provide more than minimal health, housing, and transportation services.

Political leaders and administrators in developing countries are concerned about overurbanization because it is a problem they must deal with every day. The purpose of this Public Issues paper is to contribute to an understanding of the problem by first outlining the history and nature of the policies that led to rapid urbanization. We then analyze policies that might retard the current urban growth rate in major cities by redirecting the flow of migrants to new towns and smaller cities in rural areas and by increasing the attractiveness of small-farm agriculture.

Two policy approaches, undertaken simultaneously, are necessary. The first, rural development, is now widely accepted—in theory, if not always in practice. Its aim is to increase employment and incomes in the countryside so that fewer people feel compelled to migrate in search of a livelihood. But that step is not enough, for the cities have a running head start. The subsidized jobs, incomes, and amenities of modern urban life are firmly established in one form or another in many countries. Consequently, unless urban-biased policies are gradually dismantled, rural areas and smaller cities will never become an attractive alternative to the principal urban areas. Eliminating these biases thus becomes the second component of a holistic strategy to deal with rapid city growth. This is not an argument that developing countries should remain rural and disregard industrialization. Rather, it asserts that in the absence of participatory rural development, few countries will be able to achieve their industrialization goals without severe and chronic urban problems.

In order to eliminate the urban bias in development policies, three equally dramatic and perhaps unpopular steps need to be taken. The first is to end the special tax breaks, subsidized interest rates, excessive tariff protection, and other privileges enjoyed exclusively by urban large-scale industry. The second is to modify minimum wages by holding them to the level of average agricultural incomes while simultaneously slowing the growth of urban real wages at all levels in both the public and private sector. Third, governments must curtail the expansion of urban public services and instead provide for them in rural towns and small-city service centers.

There are few alternatives to these difficult measures. Developing countries cannot depend on continued foreign aid from Western nations, which are experiencing economic problems of their own. The costs of such necessary imports as oil, food, and fertilizer have risen, while many mineral and agricultural export prices have dropped or increased only slightly. This gives poorer countries fewer resources than ever with which to finance development programs, while increasing the negative impact of costly errors.

And yet, the problem of urban growth worsens with each passing year. As Robert McNamara, president of the World Bank, said: "The cities are filling up and urban unemployment steadily grows . . . the 'marginal men,' the wretched strugglers for survival on the fringes of farm and city, may already number more than half a billion, by 1990 two billion. Can we imagine any human order surviving with so gross a mass of misery piling up at its base?"

City Bias
and Rural Neglect:
The Dilemma
of Urban Development

The Urbanization Dilemma

The cities of the developing world are growing at an extremely rapid pace. Millions of people are migrating each year from rural to urban areas, even though many of the largest cities have, for all practical purposes, given up trying to provide more than minimal sanitation, health, housing, and transportation services to their dense populations. Industrial production has expanded, but so too has urban unemployment and underemployment. In the countryside the poorest people are scarcely better off now than they were 15 years ago, and in some areas their situation has worsened.[1]

As large as these cities are today, many are destined to become substantially larger in the years to come. For example, Figure 1 shows that in 1950 about 38 percent of city dwellers lived in the developing world. By 1975, however, about the same number of developing-world people—750 million—lived in cities as those in the developed world. By the year 2000, more than two and a half times that number will populate the urban areas of the developing countries, while the cities of the industrialized world will have increased by less than 50 percent. Whereas only 16 developing-world cities had a population in excess of 4 million in 1975, by the year 2000 there will be 61. The cities of Africa are expected to grow by 336 percent, to almost 250 million population; South Asia by 298 percent, to almost 800 million; Latin America by 235 percent, to more than 450 million; and East Asia by 225 percent, to over 500 million (see Appendix, Tables A-1 and A-2).

In 1950, 11 of the world's largest cities were in the industrialized countries; in 1980 only seven were; by the year 2000, only three will be (see Figure 2). Metropolitan Mexico City will be the largest urban area in the year 2000, with about 31 million people, followed by Sao Paulo, Brazil, with 26 million, Tokyo-Yokohama with more than 24 million, New

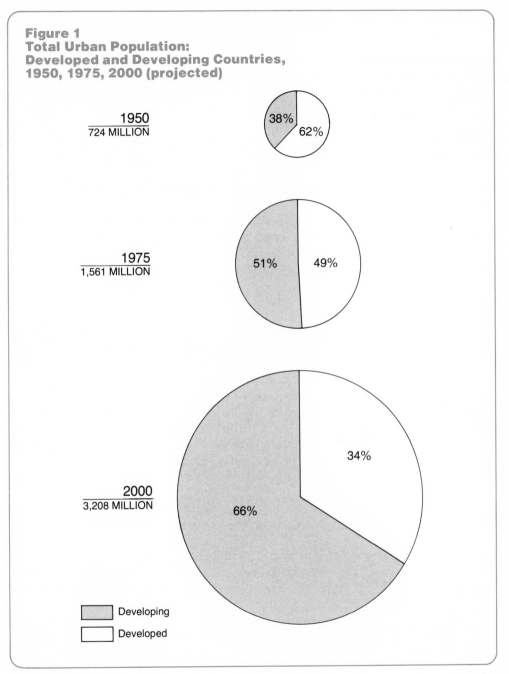

Figure 1
Total Urban Population:
Developed and Developing Countries,
1950, 1975, 2000 (projected)

1950
724 MILLION

38% 62%

1975
1,561 MILLION

51% 49%

2000
3,208 MILLION

34%

66%

Developing

Developed

3

Figure 2
The 15 Largest
Metropolitan Areas
(UN estimates
for 1980 and 2000,
in millions)

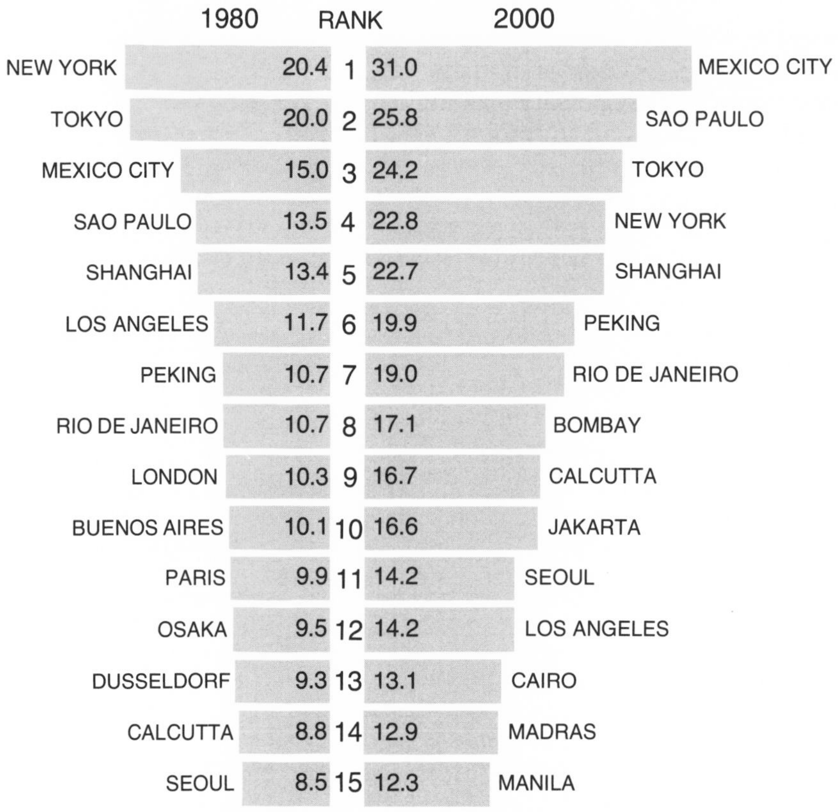

1980		RANK		2000
NEW YORK	20.4	1	31.0	MEXICO CITY
TOKYO	20.0	2	25.8	SAO PAULO
MEXICO CITY	15.0	3	24.2	TOKYO
SAO PAULO	13.5	4	22.8	NEW YORK
SHANGHAI	13.4	5	22.7	SHANGHAI
LOS ANGELES	11.7	6	19.9	PEKING
PEKING	10.7	7	19.0	RIO DE JANEIRO
RIO DE JANEIRO	10.7	8	17.1	BOMBAY
LONDON	10.3	9	16.7	CALCUTTA
BUENOS AIRES	10.1	10	16.6	JAKARTA
PARIS	9.9	11	14.2	SEOUL
OSAKA	9.5	12	14.2	LOS ANGELES
DUSSELDORF	9.3	13	13.1	CAIRO
CALCUTTA	8.8	14	12.9	MADRAS
SEOUL	8.5	15	12.3	MANILA

Source: United Nations, cited in note 8.

York with almost 23 million, and Shanghai with a slightly smaller population. Of more significance and alarm, however, are prospects for cities such as Bombay (17.1 million), Calcutta (16.7 million), Jakarta (16.6 million), Cairo (13.1 million), Madras (12.9 million), and Manila (12.3 million) where both urban services and new employment opportunities have already fallen far behind population increases.

As a specific illustration of developing-world urban population growth, consider Mexico City. In 1940 the population of Mexico City was slightly in excess of a million and a half inhabitants. This represented only 8 percent of the total Mexican population. Over the next 40 years, however, the situation changed dramatically. Between 1940 and 1950 Mexico City's population almost doubled. Significantly, over 70 percent of this increase—850,000 people—was due to internal rural-to-urban migration (with minor boundary reclassification) and only 30 percent to natural increase. In the 1950s, the city gained over 1,930,000 new inhabitants, about half of whom were migrants. In the 1960s, the population swelled to over 8.3 million as almost one and a half million new migrants arrived, twice the number of the previous decade. The massive migration into Mexico City during the period 1940–70 also provided the base for the current high level of natural increase. More than half of the city's growth during this period resulted directly or indirectly from heavy internal migration. Demographers estimate that the present Mexico City population is almost 14 million and that by the year 2000 it will reach 31 million. Although the numbers may be larger than other developing-country cities, as shown in Figure 2, Mexico City's phenomenal growth pattern is shared by a sizable proportion of Asian urban areas, with some of the most rapid growth processes only now gathering momentum in Africa.

Mexico City's phenomenal growth is shared by a sizable proportion of Asian urban areas, with some of the most rapid growth processes only now gathering momentum in Africa.

5

Given the squalid
conditions for many in the
cities, rural-to-urban
migration underscores the
dismal life in the rural
areas more than the
achievement of urban
economic growth.

It is true, as many observers have noted, that the
possibility of earning larger salaries in the cities has
been the major stimulus (although numerous noneconomic stimuli also exist) to the mass migration
from the countryside. But given the squalid conditions for many in the cities, this migration underscores the dismal life in the rural areas more
than the achievement of urban economic growth.
We are dealing here with a problem of uncontrolled urbanization, a glaring defect of economies
so preoccupied with industrial "modernization"
and so biased in their development strategies toward the urban modern sector that they are unable
to satisfy even the basic needs of their people in
either the cities or the rural areas. Excessive urbanization is also a defect of societies that have not
been able to create large enough domestic markets
to stimulate both agriculture and industry to produce more (while overseas markets in the developed countries shrink in response to economic
policies designed to protect their own local man-
ufactures). For developing nations, the policy of
neglecting agriculture, in some cases bleeding it
through resource withdrawals, has produced stagnating or inadequate income growth in rural areas,
while the policy of importing large-scale, labor-
saving technology to achieve instant industrialization has meant that urban job opportunities have
not grown as fast as the numbers seeking work.
Many thousands of rural peasants deprived of their
land by premature mechanization or crowded onto
it by rapid population growth have sought their
salvation in the rapidly growing cities, only to dis-
cover that the reality rarely reflects the image of a
significantly better life.

For developing nations,
the policy of neglecting
agriculture, in some cases
bleeding it through
resource withdrawals, has
produced stagnating or
inadequate income growth
in rural areas.

Overurbanization

Overurbanization—a situation in which cities cannot adequately provide their rapidly growing populations with basic services and reasonable job

opportunities—is not a comfortable concept among economists and planners. One reason is that it was not supposed to happen. Economists in the West and government officials in the countries that gained independence after World War II hastily searched for theoretical guidelines and practical policies to promote development. Unfortunately, they thought they had only one model—industrialization. The Soviet Union and the West differed over how to achieve industrialization, but they agreed on its vital importance. The problems of the newly independent countries seemed too severe then and now to permit the luxury of copying the slow evolutionary development of modern capitalism. The planned, forced industrialization of the Soviet Union, without its harshest measures, seemed to be a much more realistic method.

An inevitable part of industrialization is urbanization. The movement of people and resources from the countryside to the city was expected to provide the cheap labor and forced savings to stimulate urban industrialization. Then at some point it was expected that rapid urbanization, like population growth rates, would taper off, resulting in a less populated but more productive agricultural area. Rural people would then be roughly as well off as workers in the industrialized cities. Migration would slow to a trickle because the economic incentive to move would be gone.

With few exceptions industrialization did not become the engine capable of pulling a whole society to a more modern and just platform. The rough balance between the rural and urban sectors seemed as far off as ever, and to a number of economists and government leaders perhaps even impossible to achieve with policies focusing only on the growth of modern industry. By the early 1970s they began to realize that reality was not conforming to theory. Within a few years a new consensus on the most desirable development strategy emerged, empha-

Western economists and government officials in the countries that gained independence after World War II hastily searched for theoretical guidelines and practical policies to promote development. Unfortunately, they thought they had only one model—industrialization.

Industrialization rarely became the engine capable of pulling a whole society to a more modern and just platform.

sizing the role of agriculture and the importance of increasing the incomes of the poorest people in a society. To date, however, the commitment to this strategy has not been strong enough to significantly change the urbanization-industrialization policies of past decades.

Another reason for discomfort among economists and urban planners is that overurbanization cannot be precisely defined. There is no mathematical formula that stipulates a point beyond which cities should not grow. Moreover, optimal city size is a function of a wide range of economic, social, and geographic factors that vary from country to country. Presumably there is no limit to the size of a city as long as it can expand outward and upward and its industry and service sectors grow rapidly enough to absorb large numbers of new workers. In practice, however, the great majority of developing countries lack the financial resources (not to mention the organizational and planning capacity) to pursue policies of unlimited growth. Their leaders are thus deeply concerned about the geographic distribution of their population and increasingly have adopted policies to slow the rate of urbanization. For example, a United Nations survey in 1977 found that 113 of 119 developing countries considered the distribution of their population unacceptable. Some 94 countries on all continents, including South Korea, Indonesia, the Philippines, Kenya, Tanzania, Brazil, Cuba, and Venezuela, reported they had adopted policies to alter the distribution of their peoples, ranging from trying to slow or even reverse migration to the cities to lowering fertility rates. A major finding of the survey was that "the location of population is a more widespread source of government concern . . . than is natural increase or its components. The former, apparently, is more immediately linked to development means, ends and planning mechanisms than is the latter."[2]

One reason for discomfort among economists and urban planners is that overurbanization cannot be precisely defined. There is no mathematical formula that stipulates a point beyond which cities should not grow.

Because of the widespread and growing government concern over rapid urbanization, it is essential that both the population and the development community pay considerably more attention to this critical issue. Much more research is needed, but at this time there would seem to be three clear signs marking cities grown too large to fulfill their historic role in promoting developing-world economic growth. They are:

- The number of unemployed and underemployed is large and growing.

- The proportion of the urban labor force working in industry is scarcely growing and may be declining.

- The sheer numbers of people and the rate of population growth are so great that governments cannot adequately provide more than minimal health, housing, and transportation services.[3]

Research has shown that the rural poor are often simultaneously "pushed" to the cities by stagnating or declining local economic opportunities and "pulled" by expectations of abundant jobs and higher incomes. Discussions of the "pull" of the cities, however, sometimes suggest that it is primarily the bright lights or the good life that successfully lures the peasants in droves. More accurately it is a combination of rural poverty and higher expected incomes in the major cities that simultaneously stimulates rural-to-urban migration. This distinction is not simply semantical. It is made to force researchers and decision makers to focus as much attention on rural poverty as on urban growth. Only then will it be possible to devise policies more in keeping with the needs of the whole society. Moreover, it seems increasingly possible that an indirect approach to urban problems, namely through heavy investments in the rural sec-

Research has shown that the rural poor are often simultaneously "pushed" to the cities by stagnating or declining economic opportunities and "pulled" by expectations of abundant jobs and higher incomes.

tor, may have more desirable effects on alleviating urban development concerns than the usual urban-directed policies.

Many developing countries have bled agriculture to provide the resources for increasing the pace of industrialization and urbanization. This policy amounts to a significant urban bias that has become ingrained in the economic life of most developing countries.[4] Policies derived from this bias serve to widen the urban-rural expected income gap, ensuring that high rates of migration will continue despite growing urban unemployment. As long as rural incomes remain depressed and urban wages are kept artificially high by government policy and other institutional supports, rural migrants will continue to flood into the cities in search of high-paid but elusive (or illusory) urban modern sector jobs.

The experiences of the past few decades indicate that urbanization may be a necessary condition for modernization and economic development where populations are large. But it is by no means a sufficient condition. Many experts in the developing and industrialized worlds now believe that a more productive rural sector is the vital, missing ingredient. This paper argues that it will be impossible to develop the countryside unless the policies that produced overurbanization and urban bias are changed. The next step, then, is to describe these policies more fully and show how they were formulated.

The following section provides a brief history of the industrialization policies that, in combination with the neglect of the countryside, led to the massive urban migrations of the past three decades. Postwar economic development theories at first welcomed such population shifts. But the size of the migration flows was unexpected, and the level

As long as rural incomes remain depressed and urban wages are kept artificially high by government policy and other institutional supports, rural migrants will continue to flood into the cities in search of high-paid but elusive urban modern sector jobs.

did not taper off in time as economic theories predicted. Rapid migration continued because population growth in rural areas remained at high levels, rural poverty worsened, and urban wages and incomes were maintained at levels much higher than free markets would have allowed. The push and pull of these forces was so strong that migration levels were unaffected by high and growing unemployment and underemployment in the cities. Thus, the push of rural poverty and the pull of high urban incomes produced the first sign of over-urbanization: unprecedented numbers of people streaming into cities that are growing too large too fast. In the process, enormous social problems were created. Finally, this population growth in combination with the increased use of imported labor-saving technology produced the other two signs: growing urban unemployment and underemployment and a declining proportion of the labor force working in the modern industrial sector.

Rapid Industrialization: The Only Model

During their years of colonial status, many developing countries were expressly forbidden to create manufacturing industries. Britain, for example, encouraged Indians to grow cotton, but textiles had to be woven and clothing made in the mother country. One of the economic aims of colonialism was to extract natural resources from the subject areas, finish them in the mother country, and sell the goods back in the colonies. The awesome struggles of World War II involved machines as much as men, and the outcome could be interpreted as the victory of greater industrial might. Small wonder, then, that the former colonial states followed the examples of the West and the Soviet Union that equated power with industry, modernization with economic independence, and urbanization with a better life. Rapid industrialization was considered the only model for economic development.

There were, however, several important differences between the newly independent states and the developed countries on the eve of their industrialization a century or more ago. By far the most important was that of population. The rudimentary health systems introduced by European powers had sharply reduced death rates in the colonies. But birth rates remained nearly as high as before. Therefore, the populations of newly independent developing countries grew at an annual rate of 2.0 to 3.5 percent, compared with a rate of 0.5 percent in Europe during its heyday.[5] By the 1950s, of course, no country could export people to the New World as Ireland, Germany, and Italy, among others, had done over the previous century, for there was no country to accept large numbers of immigrants once the United States imposed immigration restrictions after World War I.[6]

Ironically, this great difference in population growth rates did not suggest the need for policies different from those that had been followed by the West and the Soviet Union. On the contrary, it strengthened the belief of economists and officials worldwide that more and faster industrialization was needed in the former colonies. After all, the birth rate in the West declined only after industrialization and urbanization had taken hold.

Industrialization Policies

Several economic theories were formulated in the 1950s and early 1960s to explain how the developing countries could modernize. At that time, these theories all agreed industrialization was the path to independence and freedom. Even the

Marxists did not dispute this point. Several important policies grew out of this industrialization priority, regardless of ideological orientation.

For one thing, domestic savings had to be increased and marshaled to provide the capital needed to build industry and the roads and seaports to link the (mostly foreign-owned) factories with other parts of the country and the outside world. Typically, the large agricultural base was seen as a sector from which additional income could be squeezed to support fledgling industries protected by the government from foreign competition. Protection took the form of overvaluing one's own currency so that it would be inexpensive to import the machines and technology needed to get industry going. Tariffs and quotas were imposed to prevent farmers from importing cheaper agricultural and consumer goods, forcing them to pay the relatively higher prices dictated by the high-cost, protected domestic industries. Furthermore, the overvaluation of a currency meant that export prices were artificially cheapened. Thus, there was little incentive to farmers to increase production of export crops.

One major justification for squeezing farmers and rural enterprises was the belief that they could not supply enough capital for a long-range, ongoing program of development. Rural people, it was argued, could not save as much of their incomes as could urban and industrial workers. Because rural inhabitants were poor, any additional income would be spent on necessities. Urban workers, however, could afford to save, and government could then use such monies to invest in various development projects. Business and industry owners could save a great deal more, while favorable tax treatment of profits would provide an added incentive. Therefore, a society could accumulate capital to continuously expand its output only as long as the urban

Several economic theories were formulated in the 1950s and early 1960s. These theories all agreed industrialization was the path to independence and freedom.

One major justification for squeezing farmers and rural enterprises was the belief that they could not supply enough capital for a long-range, ongoing program of development.

13

sector in general, and heavy industry in particular, kept growing. Squeezing agriculture at first to get the capital and cheap labor needed to start the industrialization process might produce suffering for a time, but it was believed to be the quickest path to a better future for the whole society. Of course, there was a model for such development—the Soviet Union.

Whatever resources governments could muster were heavily invested in creating and supporting industries. Very little went to improving agriculture. For instance, in a sample of 18 developing countries, it was found that only 12 percent of public and private investments went to agriculture during the 1950s and 1960s. Yet, agriculture produced almost 30 percent of the gross national product in these countries.[7] This low level of investment was much smaller than developed countries had placed in their rural sectors when they began to industrialize.

Meanwhile, the plant and equipment for large-scale industry had to be imported from the developed world, where over 95 percent of technological research and development takes place. One of the major aims of Western technology is to reduce dependence on labor. In developing countries, however, labor is cheap and capital expensive. Hence, a paradoxical situation arose in which scarce capital was used to purchase expensive imported equipment that saved on cheap labor.

Planners and economists realized that this incongruity would occur. It did not bother them, however, because industry and the rest of the economy, it was believed, would grow fast enough to absorb the unemployed and underemployed. In time, then, wage rates could be expected to increase so that labor-saving machinery would be economically justifiable. At any rate, there seemed to be few alternatives and little choice at the time.

Just as economic growth was unthinkable without industrialization, urbanization was believed to be a necessary and desirable by-product of modernization. There are a number of apparent economic advantages to establishing cities. Most important for developing countries is the belief that concentrating importers, manufacturers, retailers, and large numbers of consumers in one or a few areas would usually produce the most goods and services at the least cost for the largest market. Also the large labor force that gathers in a city could be expected to have the mix of skills and education to fill or be trained to fill industrial jobs. Their number would tend to keep wage rates at reasonable levels, which would help keep production costs down.

In addition, the concentration of technical and managerial skills in a city breeds innovation. Lastly, the concentration of people in a city, as opposed to their dispersal in the countryside, makes it fairly easy to reach them at lower cost with such services as roads and public transportation, schools, health clinics, and water systems.

Governments, therefore, directly encouraged city growth by subsidizing the creation and maintenance of these services. Often, too, user taxes were insufficient to cover the costs of building a network of highways linking cities with one another and with ports. Government subsidized such construction, which lowered the cost of doing business and provided an incentive for plants to locate in cities.

Most developing-country governments also indirectly encouraged the growth of the largest cities, particularly the capitals. Government plays a key role in the economic life of almost all developing countries. The concentration of decision makers and bureaucrats in the largest cities, most often in the capitals, induced producers of goods and services to locate there. Typically, the capital or a few large cities had the best, or only, transportation and communication system in the country, thus lowering the cost of production and distribution in those areas. Of course, as industry grew in a particular area it became even more attractive for new enterprises to locate there.

Rural-to-Urban Migration

Rural-to-urban migration continues to be a major contributor to the rapid growth of developing-world cities. For example, it is estimated that net migration now accounts for between one-third and three-fourths of the urban population growth in developing countries.[8] Table 1 provides some recent data on the share of urban growth due to migration for a representative group of developing countries. Some writers, however, attribute urban growth mostly to fertility levels among people already in cities. Although this may be correct statis-

Table 1
Internal Migration as a Source of Urban Growth: Selected Developing Countries, 1970–75

Country	Annual Urban Growth (percent)	Share of Growth Due to Migration (percent)
Argentina	2.0	35
Brazil	4.5	36
Colombia	4.9	43
India	3.8	45
Indonesia	4.7	49
Nigeria	7.0	64
Philippines	4.8	42
Sri Lanka	4.3	61
Tanzania	7.5	64
Thailand	5.3	45

Source: K. Newland, *City Limits: Emerging Constraints on Urban Growth*, Worldwatch Paper no. 38, Washington, D.C., August 1980, p. 10.

tically, it is misleading. Many studies have shown that the vast majority of migrants continue to be men and women in their 20s, the age group most active in forming families. Therefore, their settling in cities pushes up growth due to natural increase.[9] Directly and indirectly, then, the phenomenal growth of most developing-world cities has largely been a result of migration on a historically vast scale.[10]

Rural-to-urban migration continues to be a major contributor to the rapid growth of developing-world cities.

How rapid has urbanization been? In 1950, 16.7 percent of the developing-world population lived in cities; in 1970, the proportion was 25.8 percent; by the year 2000, it is expected to be 43.5 percent. But there is a sharp difference in the level of urbanization among regions. In 1970, for example, 22.9 percent of Africans lived in urban areas, 20.5 percent of South Asians, 28.6 percent of East Asians, but 57.4 percent of Latin Americans.

Experts and officials worldwide at first anticipated and welcomed the migration of rural people to the cities of the developing countries, for that was considered a sign that industrialization was taking root. As mentioned above, it was thought that, in time, income growth rates in the cities would level off as the labor market became saturated with migrants. Meanwhile, agricultural growth and the higher earnings of the now relatively scarce labor pool in rural areas would raise incomes to roughly balance those in the cities. This would end the stimulus to migrate. Thus, the responsiveness of labor to changing income-earning opportunities in urban and rural areas was expected to convert what seemed initially an unbalanced growth to a stable, self-correcting process.

Experts and officials worldwide at first anticipated and welcomed the migration of rural people to the cities of developing countries.

As is now evident, this never happened. The principal reasons for the failure are directly and indirectly related to the very industrialization and urbanization policies that were supposed to spur economic growth for all. First, stagnating economic conditions in rural areas ensured that population growth would continue at record high levels. Second, large population increases combined with low incomes forced more and more rural people to look around them for ways to better their condition. Third, the policy of protecting urban industry created higher incomes and more job opportunities in the cities. Other government policies—subsidizing food and legislating modern sector wage and salary scales, for example—further increased urban incomes. The result was a massive movement of people despite high and growing levels of urban unemployment and underemployment. Although some internal migration arises from noneconomic factors, including rural violence, drought, and the desire to break away from traditional role requirements, most researchers agree that the financial motive dominates.

That the growth of cities occurred within the context of an unprecedented population growth rate of 2.1 percent a year was not unexpected.[11] What was unexpected, however, was how very much faster the cities grew in comparison with the overall rate of population increase.

Although urban growth rates have been much higher than rates of increase of rural populations in recent decades, the countryside still contains many more people than the cities. Urban populations increased by an average of 4.3 percent a year between 1950 and 1970, from about 275 million to about 651 million. Rural areas grew at the much slower yearly rate of 1.6 percent during the same period. In absolute terms, however, the rural population increased from 1.4 billion to 1.9 billion. By comparison, urban growth rates in the developed world averaged 2.2 percent a year over the same period, the population increasing from 449 million to 703 million. In rural areas, however, developed-country populations declined an average of 0.2

percent a year between 1950 and 1970, from 406 million to 384 million.

The extremely high population increases in developing countries were the result of several factors. Birth rates were very high—commonly over 40 per thousand persons—throughout the developing world until the 1960s. Thereafter they dropped significantly in countries where the standard of living grew quickly, and especially where most rural inhabitants shared in the benefits of economic progress. Taiwan, South Korea, and Sri Lanka are examples of where this occurred. In these same countries, death rates dropped even more dramatically due to the widespread introduction of public health measures. The net effect, nevertheless, was to slow population growth.[12]

However, in those countries where incomes scarcely rose, or rose very unevenly, birth rates have continued at record rates while death rates have declined, but not as much as in the better-off countries. The net effect has been record high population growth. Most developing countries, including some of the largest, fit into this second category.

The result has been simply too many people to be supported by the land. The countryside in many developing nations has thus become a vast poorhouse. More than 80 percent of the estimated 750 million poor people in the developing countries live in rural areas. More than 80 million families farm less than two hectares; many of them have only slivers of land that produce incomes below the poverty level. Another 30 million families are tenants, sharecroppers, or squatters and, generally, their incomes are even lower than the first group. The very poorest, typically, are the landless who only work seasonally. Their number is growing, especially in the large Asian countries of Bangladesh, India, and Pakistan.[13]

The economic position of small farmers often wors-

In those countries where incomes scarcely rose, or rose very unevenly, birth rates have continued at record rates while death rates declined, but not as much as in the better-off countries.

More than 80 percent of the estimated 750 million poor inhabitants in the developing countries live in rural areas.

19

ened because of government neglect of agriculture. They were able to obtain little or no aid to increase production. Meanwhile, the relatively well-off farmers could afford on their own to purchase fertilizers, better seed, and the like, which increased their production and incomes. Such was the case in certain regions of India, for example, during the Green Revolution of the 1960s. Before that, the income of small farmers often was not much less than that of large farmers because the former used their large families to intensively cultivate their land. Therefore, the small farms were more productive per unit of land than the large farms, which often reduced the income difference between the two. However, the improved strains of wheat needed irrigation, and the farms and areas that had assured supplies of water were already relatively prosperous. The new seeds increased the productivity of land, so that much of the advantage traditional small farmers had over large farmers disappeared. Indeed, the Green Revolution seems to have widened income differences in India.[14]

However, both rich and poor in rural areas are harmed by government foreign exchange and domestic pricing policies designed to raise the price of manufactured goods relative to agricultural goods. One estimate is that farmers have to pay twice as much for manufactured goods as they would if they could buy the same products on the world market.[15] Another study argues that farmers and rural workers lose as much as 15 to 20 percent of their income because of the artificially high prices they have to pay for manufactured goods.[16]

Furthermore, government programs typically make it advantageous to live in the city regardless of income level. Most governments, for example, concentrate medical and education services in urban areas, and these may be free or very low-cost for poor people.[17] Subsidized food programs for the poor often are extensive in urban areas and totally inadequate in rural areas. In Bangladesh, for example, a rationing system distributes grains at low prices to the poor. Two-thirds of the country's subsidized food went to the urban poor in 1973 and 1974, even though the population of the cities (including the middle and upper classes) was only about 9 percent of the total for the country, while the number of the "extremely poor" in rural areas was two and a half times greater than the total urban population.[18]

The net effect of these public policies, as indicated earlier, was to spur population growth in the cities to unexpected levels. And if recent data from eight developing countries can be generalized, the rate of migration may be increasing. Nevertheless, some researchers point out that the rate at which cities are growing today is no more rapid than it was for the developed countries at an earlier stage of their history. They point out that the population in urban centers of developing countries rose from 16.7 percent in 1950 to 28.0 percent in 1975. In the developed world, about 17.2 percent of the total population was urbanized in 1875 and 25 years later the proportion was 26.1 percent.[19] Such a comparison could lead to an unwarranted complacency if not tempered by several considerations. First, it is a sad commentary, even if it is unavoidable, that the miserable and inhumane experiences of the working classes of the West are being repeated 75 years later in other parts of the world. Very little, then, has changed. Second, it is more likely that the poverty of large numbers of people will be deeper and longer lasting today than ever before because there are so many more of the poor and the population increases are unprecedented. Third, urban employment growth is lagging far behind urban population growth in today's developing countries in comparison with the historic experience of Western nations. The *rate* of urbanization

In Bangladesh in 1973–74, two-thirds of the country's subsidized food went to the urban poor, even though the population of the cities was only about 9 percent of the national total.

The *rate* of urbanization may be no greater than it has always been, but the sheer numbers involved mock any notion that economic development is proceeding on target.

21

may be no greater than it always has been, but the sheer numbers of people involved and the depth of their poverty mock any notion that economic development is proceeding on target.

Unemployment
in Industry

As rural-to-urban migration accelerated, people were seeking jobs in industries that increasingly needed fewer of them. The kind of industry that was imported from the West and the Soviet Union after World War II could not possibly grow fast enough to keep up with the sudden increases in population. This situation was very different from that faced by the West when it began to industrialize more than a century ago. In the early phase of the Industrial Revolution during the late eighteenth and nineteenth centuries, the division of labor cut production costs much more than the simple machinery then in existence. In addition, the machinery first introduced on the farms and in factories used a good deal of labor.[20] Only after the revolution gained momentum, as inventions multiplied, did entrepreneurs find the long-run cost of borrowing money or using their own profits to purchase machinery to be cheaper than hiring the labor necessary to produce the same amount of goods. Whenever possible, therefore, factory owners began substituting machinery for labor, particularly in the high-wage environment of the United States.

The kind of industry that was imported from the West and the Soviet Union after World War II could not possibly grow fast enough to keep pace with the sudden increases in population.

The shift from labor-intensive to capital-intensive manufacturing took enough time in the West for rural migrants to be absorbed by industry. Although the transfer was not achieved without suffering, industry, even though it became increasingly capital-intensive, generally expanded quickly enough to absorb almost all who wanted to work. In some countries where industry did not grow sufficiently for an increasing population, people migrated overseas. The movement to North America and Australasia at times seemed to resemble an evacuation.[21] By the end of World War II, however, technology was far advanced in using less labor, and large-scale international migration was no longer legally possible. An important "safety valve" for the rural poor and the urban unemployed was therefore eliminated. As a study by the World Bank reported of the technology currently being imported by today's developing countries: "The enclaves of capital-intensive, relatively automated, large-scale industries with advanced technologies . . . are thus not contributing sufficiently to stable and reliable employment growth."[22] By way of illustration, manufacturing output grew two to six times faster than manufacturing employment in the great majority of developing countries between 1963 and 1975.

The low labor-absorptive capacity of modern industry means that more of it is not the answer to the employment problems of developing countries. In most of these countries, the modern industrial sector employs 10 to 20 percent of the total labor force.[23] Even assuming the larger figure, to absorb an increase of 2.5–3 percent a year in the labor force, industry would have to expand 12.5–15 percent a year ($20\% \times 12.5\% = 2.5\%$; $20\% \times 15\% = 3\%$). The total labor force is expected to grow between 2.4 and almost 3 percent a year in various parts of Africa, Asia, and Latin America for the rest of the century. But there are very few instances of industrial employment growing between 12.5 and 15 percent a year. Such high growth is now virtually impossible to achieve because of the labor-saving nature of modern industry.

It should be no surprise, then, that unemployment and underemployment rates are high and chronic

The shift from labor-intensive to capital-intensive manufacturing took enough time in the West for rural migrants to be absorbed by industry.

in the cities of developing countries. Figures on urban unemployment and especially underemployment are very sketchy, but they suggest the unemployment rate was about 10 to 15 percent in the mid-1970s, totaling some 100 million people. Another 30 percent, or more than 300 million people, were believed to be considerably underemployed. In Africa, urban unemployment rates as high as 20 percent are not uncommon. In Latin America, almost half of the cities with unemployment figures have rates between 10 and 20 percent. In Asia, rates between 7 and 14 percent are common.

In such situations of high unemployment, traditional economic theory teaches that wages should fall. Actually, unemployment would not need to be high for this to happen because there is always a surplus of workers in developing countries pressing for the privileged jobs in modern industry. Contrary to theory, however, the price of labor does not drop, for workers in the modern sector are usually well organized. Unionized workers will, of course, not only resist any lowering of wages, but also strive for increases despite unemployment or the ample supply of potential competing workers. Even if they are not unionized, modern sector workers are normally protected from outright exploitation by minimum wage and fringe benefits laws. In either case, wages cannot fall below a particular level, and they normally increase in step with or in excess of the rate of inflation. This is another incentive to the industrialist to invest in labor-saving machinery.

The unemployment problem is so huge because the urban labor force is expanding at the rate of 4 to 7 percent a year while job opportunities are increasing by only 2.5 percent a year. The lack of jobs is particularly severe for 15- to 24-year-olds, who because they generally are better educated than their elders are inclined to hold out for the highest paying jobs in the modern sector. Their rate of unemployment is almost double that for the labor force as a whole.[24]

Moreover, 30 to 50 percent of the total work force in many countries is in service occupations[25]—sometimes called the urban "informal" sector. This category includes, in addition to domestics, taxi drivers, and hotel workers, the innumerable street hawkers, shoeshiners, and day laborers so commonly seen in the cities. The very opposite occurred in the developed countries when they were industrializing—the bulk of people displaced from farms went into industry. Also unlike the industrialized countries, economic development is occurring at higher levels of urbanization. For example, the countries that developed earliest—England, France, and the United States—did so at lower levels of urbanization than those that developed later—Germany, Japan, and the Soviet Union. They in turn developed at lower levels of urbanization than now exist in the developing world.

Additionally, in some areas, particularly Latin America, a higher percentage of people are living in cities and a lower percentage are finding jobs in manufacturing than was true at comparable stages of economic development in the countries now industrialized. In 1900, for example, an estimated 21.6 percent of the total labor force of the developed countries worked in industry while 26.1 percent of the population lived in cities. In 1970, Central Africa was almost as urbanized but only 9.5 percent of the labor force worked in industry; North Africa was more urbanized while 15.8 percent of labor was employed in industry; the Caribbean, tropical South America, and temperate South America were much more urbanized (45.1, 53.9, 56.1 percent) while their labor force was not quite as heavily engaged in manufacturing (21.1, 21.4, 19.6 percent); western Asia was much more urbanized (44.5 percent) but only 18.4 percent were employed in industry. The only area that was both more urbanized and had a greater percentage of its work force in manufacturing was East Asia (South Korea and Taiwan, for example, but not China), with 47.7 percent of the population urbanized and 25.4 percent of the labor force in industry.[26]

Some argue that the industrial employment and urbanization experiences of the developed countries should not be considered the norm.[27] Rather, the experiences of today's developing countries are more like what should be expected in the course of economic development. Nevertheless, there seems to be general agreement that the capital-intensive nature of modern industrial technology precludes the absorption of anticipated large annual increases in the urban work force and that industry will not employ as large a share of labor as it once had at comparable levels of development and urbanization. Perhaps the "informal" service sector can fill the gap. This is doubtful, however, because service sector growth depends heavily on modern sector expansion. Moreover, data showing sizable increases in urban unemployment and underemployment reveal the limited nature of productive informal sector activities.

It is also quite possible that overurbanization may get worse. For one thing, there is some evidence that migration rates are increasing. If so, this would raise the proportion of the population living in the cities. Second, migration is heaviest to those cities that are already the largest. The developing world's 10 largest cities are growing more rapidly than other cities.[28] The proportion of people living in cities larger than one million grew from 19.5 to 29.3 percent from 1950 to 1975 while the share for small and medium cities dropped.[29] It is not only the supposed economic advantage of size that causes the biggest to become bigger. The largest

There is general agreement that the capital-intensive nature of modern technology cannot absorb the large annual increases in the work force.

manufacturers, importers, merchants, and distributors located in the largest cities tend to have a dominant voice in making domestic and international economic policies. It is in their interest to perpetuate and strengthen the trade and foreign exchange policies that have concentrated wealth and power in the urban centers they helped to create. Their actions may stunt the growth not only of agriculture but also of smaller cities and towns, which have a great potential for labor-intensive industry.[30]

The rapid growth of cities has far outpaced the ability of developing-country governments to provide adequate services, and many no longer try to do so. The kinds of problems that exist in the cities of the developed world exist to an even greater extent in the developing world. And the larger the city, the more frequently the problems seem to become compounded. There is evidence that air pollution, noise levels, congestion, crime, and health problems tend to increase more than proportionately with the size of urban centers.[31]

Some economists and government officials believe that with more resources, better management, and stronger growth of the informal sector, cities could provide a better life for their population. Some urban planners still argue that there is no such thing as overurbanization because cities are far more efficient than rural areas in providing employment and higher incomes, and that the alternatives—"overruralization," for example—are worse. They are too optimistic. For one thing, inflation in the industrialized countries has greatly increased the cost to many developing countries of importing enough food to feed their people, and the cost to all of importing machinery. At the same time, slower economic growth in the West and new trade

The Impact of Rapid Growth on Urban Services

The rapid growth of cities has far outpaced the ability of developing-country governments to provide adequate services, and many no longer try to do so.

27

restrictions have reduced the demand for the industrial products of the developing world. The rapid climb in the price of oil has further weakened the economic position of the developing countries. All of these factors exacerbate already serious balance-of-payments and debt service problems and constrain a developing economy's ability to maintain the existing pace of urban employment growth— let alone accelerate it.

If overurbanization has become common, self-perpetuating, and self-defeating, forcing people to remain in the countryside is not the answer. Migration, after all, is often a desperate attempt to obtain a bare minimum standard of living. People "vote" with their feet. For many developing nations, there seems to be no practical alternative to the strategy of concentrating on the development of rural areas. Migration will drop and incomes rise in the countryside only if agriculture and related small-scale rural manufacturing create more employment and higher incomes. Such an approach indirectly and slowly attacks the causes of overurbanization.

Rural poverty forces people to seek alternatives to their desperate conditions. A recent study of 27 Asian and Latin American countries concluded that where population increases were rapid, and the land crowded or very unevenly distributed, migration to cities would be high.[32] An extreme case of unequal land distribution was found in Colombia, where 0.6 percent of all farms contained 40 percent of all agricultural land, while 63 percent contained less than 5 percent of available land. In Asia, extremely high land densities are typical.

Those fortunate enough to get full-time jobs in the cities earn much more than they could have in rural areas. But these jobs are relatively scarce and the competition severe. Nevertheless, the combination of almost hopeless conditions on the land and the

For many developing nations, there seems to be no practical alternative to the strategy of concentrating on rural development.

Those fortunate enough to get full-time jobs in the cities earn much more than they could have in rural areas. But these jobs are relatively scarce and the competition severe.

possibility of getting more coveted jobs propels migrants to the cities even though many are realistic enough to expect only marginal part-time work at first. They fill the ranks of the urban informal sector. Some of these activities are genuinely productive—making and repairing household furniture and other consumer goods, for example. Others are very unproductive and often parasitic—street hawking, prostitution, car-watching, selling discarded materials, and the like. Although the informal sector provides a useful outlet for otherwise unemployed and surplus urban workers, its absorptive capacity in terms of genuinely productive activities is limited by the size and growth of urban large-scale industry. Contrary to the claims of some hopeful observers, growth of the informal sector is not a panacea for urban unemployment.

Creating a Rural Development Strategy

By the early 1970s it had become clear that the industrialization policies were not working as well as had been expected. Despite an impressive record of economic growth during the previous two decades, many developing countries seemed to have as many problems as they had started with. But it was poverty—widespread, persistent, dehumanizing, and seemingly so unnecessary in a world so rich—that riveted the attention of observers. Economic growth, where it occurred, seemed to have no effect on hundreds of millions of people who continued to go hungry every day.

By the mid-1970s, dissatisfaction had crystallized into an alternative approach—rural-based development. Its intellectual foundations were supplied by a rereading of the economic history of the West and by research that indicated for the first time that the rural sector could take a leading role in income and employment creation.

Research indicated for the first time that the rural sector could take a leading role in income and employment creation.

29

History Reread

Neither Europe, the United States, nor later Japan neglected agriculture in a rush to industrialize. By the time the cotton industry came to Lancashire and the woolen industry to Yorkshire, market towns, credit and marketing services for farmers, and local, small-scale manufacturing and commercial enterprises were established throughout England.[33]

In the United States, canals and railroads reached out to the rich farmlands of the Midwest by the mid-nineteenth century. Market towns, railroad centers, and cities grew up in the interior. In Japan, extensive land reform in the late nineteenth century led to a spurt in agricultural productivity, while technical and cooperative services were established for small farmers and artisans. Small industrial firms became manufacturing pacesetters. The transformation of the economy by World War I was accomplished under some conditions identical with those existing today in many developing countries—growing population pressures, a lack of new agricultural land, and the impossibility of relieving the situation by international migration (as had happened in Europe).

Unexpected Findings

Research began turning up some surprising findings that questioned the prevailing conventional wisdom on industrialization. For example, it was discovered that protected urban industries often contributed very little to economic growth; that higher rates of rural economic growth did not have to be achieved at the expense of a more equitable distribution of income; and that small farmers often were more productive than large ones. These conclusions buttressed the emerging argument for switching priorities from industrialization to agriculture and rural development.

Research began turning up some surprising findings that buttressed the emerging argument for switching priorities from industrialization to agriculture and rural development.

Although taxes, exchange rates, and tariffs were frequently manipulated to stimulate and protect urban industry, very often industry's contribution to economic growth was small when public subsidies and protective measures were subtracted from its output. In some cases the net contribution was barely positive. One well-known example of this occurred in Pakistan in the mid-1960s, where 6.6 percent of total domestic expenditures took the form of subsidies to large-scale industry financed by an implicit tax on agriculture (in the form of low price ceilings on farm produce). It was calculated that these industries added the equivalent of 7.0 percent of public expenditures a year to national growth. Their net contribution, therefore, was only 0.4 percent of the national budget. Their employment contribution was even less significant.

It had generally been believed that national growth depended primarily on a small segment of high-income groups being willing and able to save and invest in industry. In practice, however, the wealthy did not invest heavily in domestic industry. They often preferred to import luxury goods, travel abroad, or avoid risks by hoarding gold and jewelry. Meanwhile, higher incomes for the great bulk of poor people were almost immediately transferred into greater demand for locally produced food and simple consumer goods. Not only did this stimulate domestic production, and hence employment, but the productivity of the poor workers improved as their undernourishment declined.

A related finding, also unexpected, was that farmers were very frugal. In fact, they tended to save more than urbanites at similar levels of income.[34] The theory that the poor cannot contribute the investments necessary for growth, combined with the fact that most poor people live in rural areas, provided an important justification for the view that agriculture could not lead a society out of underdevelopment. But since income levels were more equitable in rural than urban areas, these research findings indicated that the countryside could play a far more important role than it had previously been assigned.

Other studies found that small farms were often more productive than large farms. In such diverse countries as Argentina, Brazil, Egypt, parts of India, Taiwan, and South Korea, farmers and their families on comparatively small plots spent more time and effort than larger families in getting maximum yield from the fields.[35] Just as capital-intensive industry could no longer be perceived as the panacea for development, the new thinking began to consider the highly mechanized agriculture in the West and the Soviet Union as inappropriate for the developing world.

Finally, developing-world population growth accelerated at an unexpected and alarming pace during the 1960s. Although there was considerable discussion about how to feed the growing multitude, not much was done about it. Developing-country governments discouraged talk about population explosions and their implications. By the mid-1970s, however, following drought in various parts of the world and skyrocketing prices of food, fertilizers, and fuel, the huge problem of how to provide minimal diets to hundreds of millions of people could no longer be avoided.

Despite a few good crop yields at the end of the 1970s, the future does not look promising. Trends in population, income, and agricultural output indicate that the gap between production and demand for food will increase from the 37 million metric tons in the relatively good year of 1975 to 120–145 million metric tons by 1990. Moreover, economic conditions in the poorest countries are

Just as capital-intensive industry could no longer be perceived as the panacea for development, the new thinking began to consider the highly mechanized agriculture in the West and the Soviet Union inappropriate for the developing world.

expected to worsen. In order to maintain their barely adequate nutritional standards of 1975, these countries—which contain two-thirds of the people in the market economies of the developing world—would have to grow 35 million more metric tons of food by 1990 than trends indicate is possible.[36]

The food/population dilemma provides another important reason for shifting resources to the rural areas. Even if fertility rates were somehow to drop drastically, population still would double in many developing countries because of the large numbers of young couples entering their childbearing years. Agricultural development cannot be permitted to lag if starvation and chronic undernourishment are to be avoided.

During the 1970s the new rural development strategy was being embraced by a number of leading public figures. Such developing-world spokespeople as Indira Ghandi, Luis Echeverria, and Julius Nyerere were calling for greater agricultural development. For example, at a World Conference on Agrarian Reform and Rural Development in 1979, President Nyerere of Tanzania declared: "An effective attack on world poverty can only be made by going directly to the rural areas and dealing with the problems. . . . A policy of rural development is a policy of national development." Robert McNamara began shifting the funds of the World Bank from industrialization and urban projects to agriculture and rural development. In 1973, the late Senator Hubert H. Humphrey led a successful effort to move the US Foreign Aid bill closer to the objectives of the new rural development approach. This approach has had a continuing and significant impact on developing-world planning, and its key components merit our further attention.

Even if fertility rates were somehow to drop drastically, population still would double in many developing countries because of the large numbers of young couples entering their childbearing years.

33

While emphases or particular points may differ and many important details are still being worked out, considerable agreement has emerged in recent years on the general principles of the rural development strategies.

- Growth with equity is the overall goal. Improving the income of the rural poor is as important as general economic growth.

- Agriculture must receive the highest priority. Resources and trained manpower must be poured into a sustained effort to increase food production.

- Small farmers can be the key to a successful drive to expand agricultural production if they are given low-cost access to fertilizers, water, better seeds, and credit and extension service while being accorded a fair price for their produce. Extensive mechanization is neither necessary nor desirable.

- Land reform may often be necessary to provide peasants with a greater incentive to produce more. It would also lead to a more equitable distribution of rural income and wealth.

- Rural infrastructure—roads, food-storage facilities—must be built so that farmers can easily sell their crops, which in turn could be distributed with minimum spoilage.

- Linking farmers with markets is essential. Marketing, cooperative, and financial institutions serving farmers need to be established in conveniently located market towns and small cities. Secondary schools and technical colleges should also be located there.

- Labor-intensive, small-scale manufacturing activities should be encouraged in these centers in order to increase employment while producing goods and services of use to farmers.

- More research and development is needed on technologies that efficiently use more labor and less capital in both agriculture and light industry.

- Participation in decision making must be open to people of all income levels in areas that directly affect them at both the national and community levels.

These principles interlock to form a systematic approach to the major socioeconomic problems of developing countries, but they fall short of a sufficiently comprehensive strategy for dealing with the urban dilemma. If urban population growth is to be reduced and diverted to towns and smaller cities and the living conditions in rural areas are to improve, the artificial advantages of cities must be eliminated. As long as income-earning opportunities in the two sectors remain substantially out of balance, migration will continue and the problems associated with rapid urbanization will intensify.

If urban population growth is to be reduced and living conditions in rural areas are to improve, the artificial advantages of cities must be eliminated.

Practical Policies

To cope with problems of rapid urbanization, governments in developing countries must first modify or eliminate past policies that artificially promoted urban population growth. The industrialization policies of the past not only failed to pull societies out of their state of underdevelopment, but often exacerbated problems of high unemployment and underemployment, widespread poverty, mass migration, and uncontrolled urban growth. By creating economic advantages for industries using modern labor-saving equipment, governmental urban-industrial biases have continued to frustrate a more equitable pattern of growth long after the theory supporting them has been largely repudiated by experience.

Political leaders and administrators will have to make some hard choices, many of which will be politically unpopular. They cannot neglect to extend at least minimal health and education services to poor people in the shanty towns on the edge of a megalopolis. But despite what little is often done, it is usually much more than a rural area could expect to receive. These additional public services—even though minimal compared with actual needs—are one more factor making life in the city better than in the stagnating countryside.

Thus, policies to accommodate the needs of the urban poor (not to mention the upper and middle classes, who typically receive the bulk of government largesse) are ultimately self-defeating. Far better are policies that encourage people to stay in rural areas because health, education, and incomes are improving there faster than in the cities. This would not only ease pressures to migrate, but may also be the only way, over time, to substantially lower rural birth rates. The poor generally have the largest families in rural areas. Children are their only economic asset. But as real incomes rise above minimal levels, parents begin to consider the financial advantages of having fewer children and birth rates begin to decline. A declining birth rate also seems to result from policies that promote a more equitable distribution of income.[37] Examples of countries where this happened even before the establishment of formalized family planning programs are Taiwan, Hong Kong, South Korea, and Sri Lanka. The knowledge that more children will survive, combined with the opportunity to share in the benefits of national economic growth, seems to provide the motivation to have fewer children.

Governmental urban-industrial biases have continued to frustrate a more equitable pattern of growth long after the theory supporting them has been largely repudiated by experience.

Government efforts in rural development should concentrate on creating the physical and economic climate that would reward initiatives taken by small businessmen and farmers.

Government efforts in the area of rural development should therefore concentrate on creating the physical and economic climate that would reward initiatives taken by small businesses and farmers, while continuing to provide the infrastructure necessary for a more balanced geographic development. Attempts to "fine tune" policies would probably be impractical and costly. There is a very real challenge in translating broad principles into practical programs and projects.

2 Policies to Counter Rapid Urbanization

Many of the specific policies considered in this section have been implemented in scattered countries during the past few years. It is too early to judge their success or failure. Others, such as ending the distortions in the prices of capital and labor, have been widely discussed but rarely tried. In almost all cases, insufficient attention has been given to the interrelationships of policies, the timing of their introduction, and their political feasibility.

Choosing and Timing Policies

A good program by itself can make matters worse: a widespread formal educational system without competitive job opportunities in the countryside, for example, would probably encourage increased migration. Some policies will not work without complementary measures: an urban dispersal program would not be possible without a good transportation network. Too many projects failed in the past because their economic and social implications were not considered or their results were totally unforeseen. In some cases, problems were created because of the success of a program: the Green Revolution raised food production in parts of India, but also landlessness and income inequalities; the Aswan Dam in Egypt provided needed irrigation but also created numerous public health problems. Packages of properly phased, complementary policies would be of most help to decision makers.

A good program by itself can make matters worse: a widespread formal educational system without competitive job opportunities in the countryside, for example, would probably encourage increased migration.

Some programs, such as land reform, are vital to achieving growth and equity in certain countries but they are blocked by powerful opponents. Other countries that have legislated land reform have failed to fully implement it. Holding the line on the growth of urban modern sector wages would be opposed by unions. Steps that generate intense opposition may have to wait until later in the development process. Often, however, there is no time to delay. In such cases, a well-designed series of practical policies aimed at developing the country-

40

side might rapidly create enough mass support to push through more fundamental changes. Any set of recommendations to policymakers, therefore, would be of greatest help if it started with the politically feasible and economically broad and progressed to the difficult and narrow.

For example, programs of regional development—providing rural public works and rural business aid, promoting small-farm agricultural development, providing special help for women, expanding rural education and health services, and decentralizing government decision making—may be the most practical beginning in many countries. Subsequently, governments could initiate programs to disperse urban industry as part of a regional development plan, to freeze real wages and living conditions in the urban centers, to aggressively promote appropriate technology for industry and agriculture, to colonize unused areas, and to redistribute land. Some opposition can be expected to any fundamental reform. But with the momentum of past achievements, the resistance may be less vehement than in the case of rapid, radical change.

The order of the policies recommended below reflects to a certain extent their interrelatedness. However, there is no intention here to create another "stages of growth" theory in which a country must move step by step from one policy to the next. Some countries have already initiated several programs mentioned, but not others. In certain countries practical considerations would dictate an entirely different sequence. What is appropriate for Brazil or India is unlikely to be relevant for Nigeria or Guatemala. The following recommendations, therefore, are intended merely to form a generalized package of complementary policies that need to be adapted to a nation's particular structural and economic conditions. Hence, the discussion will be brief, with references to the extensive literature on

A well-designed series of practical policies aimed at developing the countryside might create enough mass support to push through more fundamental changes.

In certain countries practical considerations would dictate an entirely different sequence of policies. What is appropriate for Brazil or India is unlikely to be relevant for Nigeria or Guatemala.

each point for those who would like more detail. Although there is no intention to gloss over some of the significant political opposition that many of the following policy recommendations will provoke in various developing countries, our major goal here is to suggest broad areas of action and to leave it to public officials and policymakers in specific countries to ascertain the political feasibility of each proposal.

The focus is first on short-term policies, those that can have a more immediate—say three- to five-year—impact on rural-urban economic imbalances. These include efforts to promote regional development, rural public works, rural nonfarm development, the dismantling of urban capital-goods biases, small-farm agricultural development, women's economic roles and activities, expanded rural education and health services, and increased government decentralization. An examination of long-term policies to stimulate dispersed urbanization, appropriate technology development for industry and agriculture, new colonization, land reform, and the elimination of urban wage biases concludes our policy review and recommendations.

Regional Development

The aim of this set of policies is to develop a network of towns and smaller cities in which small enterprises, relying chiefly on labor, would process and distribute agricultural produce and manufacture the equipment and simple consumer goods needed by small farmers.

More ambitious steps of dispersing industry and government would, of course, create jobs in smaller cities and, in the long run, slow migration to the major urban centers. In the past, rural migrants often moved to the nearest towns and cities before proceeding to a metropolitan center. However, with the growth of transportation and communication systems many migrants now move directly to the principal city.

Although absolutely essential, the rural-based regional development strategy alone cannot right the substantial urban-rural economic imbalance that now exists in many countries. There are two cutting edges to future development: rural areas must be made more attractive, while urban centers must become relatively less appealing. The first is the task of a rural-based strategy. The second requires dismantling the costly policies that make high incomes and social amenities so much more prevalent in urban areas.

Even the most dynamic of regional and agricultural development programs would probably have a minimal short-term effect on migration rates or directions because the built-in population increases are so large and poverty so widespread. In time, however, an effective set of policies could begin to direct migrants away from overurbanized metropolitan areas to rural towns and smaller regional cities. A network of employment information offices in the largest cities and rural areas might direct rural migrants and residents of the overurbanized centers to the smaller cities.

Regional development should include rural public works, rural nonfarm development, and dispersed urbanization. The last program could be delayed until the first two have started. Several rural development and dispersed urbanization programs have been started over the past few years, but it is too early to make definitive evaluations. Rural public works programs have been under way for many years in a number of countries. If what has been built can be tied in with what is planned, so much the better.

Experience has revealed numerous problems with regional development programs in various na-

There are two cutting edges to future development: rural areas must be made more attractive while urban centers become relatively less appealing.

Regional development should include rural public works, rural nonfarm development, and dispersed urbanization.

tions.[38] First, costs may be high, preventing the creation of a national program. The lowest income countries may have to work in one or two regions at a time. Other countries, including some of the low-income ones, may find that eliminating the subsidies to heavy industry will give them the additional resources to initiate a comprehensive regional development effort.

Second, too often programs do not advance beyond the construction of stop-gap public works projects, the easiest and most politically popular activity. There will not be a permanent improvement in the lives of the poor unless the creation of infrastructure helps stimulate more permanent employment opportunities in an expanding agricultural and rural business sector.

Finally, local political leaders may become enthusiastic backers of regional development as they realize that funds and projects might be distributed in their areas. Careful planning and project evaluation can thus become secondary to political expediency and local pressure group activities.

The limited experience of regional development indicates that it would be best to give one body the responsibility for carrying out or overseeing the program. A government-sponsored regional development corporation is one possibility. Another is an agency created to coordinate the work of the ministries that deal with various aspects of the program.

It is essential that private initiative be encouraged as part of the overall program. Rural entrepreneurs have become active where government did not purposely or inadvertently create obstacles to private investment.

It is essential that private initiative be encouraged as part of the overall program. Rural entrepreneurs have become active where government did not purposely or inadvertently create obstacles to private investment. For example, seasonal markets sprang up in Sierra Leone in the mid-1970s to sell agricultural produce to middlemen for resale in the

44

cities.[39] A similar development took place in the
Malagasy Republic. In Kenya's Central Province
during the 1960s, villages began evolving into
towns offering a wide range of services, all in the
absence of government over-regulation or economic power concentrated in the hands of a few.

Rural Public Works

Unlike many past rural public works programs,
more emphasis needs to be placed on smaller projects that create local employment and infrastructure. At least 15 developing countries have invested
heavily in such programs; an evaluation of the one
in Morocco indicated that 60,000 man-years of employment had been created annually, income was
being redistributed to the poor, and the rate of
return on investment was about 9 percent.[40] The
study concluded the projects were cost-effective,
output equaled that of other investments, and
wages were recycled because workers increased
their consumption of local goods and services.

Three major types of rural public works projects
are road construction, irrigation and water supply
systems, and markets and storage facilities. Many
rural areas need three types of roads.[41] First, farmers need simple paths to enable them to move to
and from their fields; such paths also stimulate clus-
tering into villages. If farmers have to live scattered,
the cost of providing them with various services
would often be prohibitive. Second, villages must
be linked to a district market, where enough buyers
and sellers can meet to avert monopolistic or mo-
nopsonistic conditions. Finally, "truck" roads are
needed to link markets to one another so that a
wheat-growing district, for example, can receive
vegetables from another area, and vice versa. Thai-

Unlike many past rural
public works programs,
more emphasis needs to
be placed on smaller
projects that create local
employment and
infrastructure.

land, the Philippines, India, Nigeria, and Malaysia among others have such coordinated road-building programs.

Irrigation is one of the principal methods of increasing production, and in some areas a quick and inexpensive method is to sink tubewells to tap groundwater. Other small projects could include construction of a village water supply and buffalo ponds. Ethiopia, Bangladesh, Malaysia, Thailand, Colombia, Bolivia, and Ecuador have programs to assist local communities to undertake such projects.

Several studies have shown that markets and storage facilities reduce the variability of foodstuff prices, speculation, and the influence of large landowners, thus improving the income of small farmers.[42] Mexico, Malaysia, and India have been building markets, while Bolivia, Malaysia, Mexico, Pakistan, Taiwan, and several African countries have storage construction programs.

Rural Nonfarm Development

The principal aim here is to encourage the expansion of the manufacturing and service sectors seeking to meet the needs of rural residents. Developing countries, international organizations, and aid-giving nations have become increasingly interested in rural development as new research found that small business could generate employment and profits. Rural development, in tandem with agricultural development, is often seen as a major means of achieving growth and equity.

Rural enterprises produce for a market that is generally dispersed and poor. Therefore, they are usually small (fewer than five employees), dispersed, and use cheap labor and the simplest, if any, machines. Their fate is closely tied to that of agriculture. One estimate is that for every increase in

Rural development, in tandem with agricultural development, is often seen as a major means of achieving growth and equity.

agricultural income in regions that are moderniz-
ing, there is a more than proportionate growth in
the demand of farmers for the products and services of local enterprise.

It is not difficult to understand why this should be.
As agriculture expands and modernizes, farmers
need more and better seeds, tools, fertilizers, and
credit services. Larger crops mean more processing, transporting, and marketing. In addition, as
earning a livelihood from farming becomes a real
possibility, families spend more time on purely agricultural work and less on producing the simple
goods and services they need. They use their increased incomes to purchase textiles or clothing, or
to hire an artisan to repair a field or household
implement.

There is some evidence that small farmers and
landless agricultural workers patronize local small
businesses more than large farmers do. The latter
may be more interested in the machines and tractors produced in urban centers or abroad.

Not surprisingly, rural and small-town nonfarm
employment varies with the level of economic development.[43] In Africa, about two-thirds of all employment off the farm is in rural villages and towns,
about one-half to two-thirds in South and East Asia,
and about one-third in Latin America. Another illustration of the importance of rural business is the
fact that it provides more employment in manufacturing than the large plants in urban centers. In
Sierra Leone, for example, 86 percent of all manufacturing employment and 95 percent of all establishments are in the countryside. In Bangladesh,
70 percent of all manufacturing jobs are in rural
areas, in Malaysia 63 percent, and in India 57 percent, the proportion dropping to 32 percent in
fairly well-developed South Korea.[44] The figures
probably underestimate the truth because it is

One illustration of the
importance of rural
enterprises is the fact that
they provide more
employment in
manufacturing than the
large plants in urban
centers.

47

much more difficult to count many small, dispersed establishments in rural areas than large plants in cities.

Where small rural enterprises have survived in the developing world, there is some evidence that they use capital more efficiently than large firms. Comparisons of enterprises indicate that the output per unit of capital is greater in smaller than in larger establishments.[45] Thus, the same enterprises that use relatively more of the plentiful factor, labor, also most efficiently use the scarce factor, capital.

Output per unit of capital is greater in smaller than in larger establishments. Additionally, small rural enterprises often have higher profit rates than large urban firms.

Additionally, small rural enterprises often have higher profit rates than large urban firms. One recent study concluded that "there is no empirical evidence to support. . . [the] contention that the profit, savings, and reinvestment rates of small-scale or rural nonfarm enterprises are necessarily lower than those of large, capital-intensive enterprises."[46]

The World Bank has found that control by local residents and officials has given nonfarm development projects the flexibility needed to properly integrate activities and to modify them as conditions change.[47] Local participation is especially important in selecting a town to be a market center, where government and cooperative services would be clustered. Although at least 20 countries reported having nonfarm development programs with a great deal of local participation, only those in Bangladesh, Niger, Malaysia, and Senegal seem to have paid the idea more than lip service.[48]

Control by local residents and officials has given nonfarm development projects the flexibility to properly integrate activities and to modify them as conditions change.

Eliminating Urban Capital-Goods Biases

As long as people expect incomes to rise faster in cities than in rural areas, they will continue to migrate in search of economic improvement. A fundamental aim of development policy, therefore, must be to increase income and job opportunities in rural areas. Not generally recognized, however, is the other side of the equation—eliminating the costly subsidies that spur the growth of a relatively few well-paid jobs in the cities. Governments need to resist pressures to further accelerate urban industrial growth in order to give rural areas a chance to catch up. Positive steps would include barring or permitting only minor increases in modern sector wages and public salary scales. More important and politically more feasible is the removal of measures that lower the effective price of capital goods. These include (1) artificially low interest rates, (2) discriminatory tariffs, (3) overvalued foreign exchange rates, and (4) special tax privileges for urban industrialists.

Interest Rates   The cost of borrowing money is often kept artificially low, particularly for large firms. Such low interest rates result from government policies that legislate interest ceilings at levels much below market rates, ostensibly to encourage investment. These rates can be especially low during inflation. For example, if the inflation rate exceeds the maximum interest rate allowed by law, the "real" rate of interest is negative. Banks, therefore, must be very cautious and keep their costs as low as possible. Typically, their safest and most cost-effective investments are in large firms, urban real estate ventures, and the like. Private banks cannot be expected to take the risk or absorb the cost of lending to many small firms in scattered parts of the country unless rates are more realistic and some type of government loan guarantees are provided. In the meantime, these rural and small-city enterprises must borrow from traditional moneylenders, whose interest rates are much higher than those of banks. In data collected for 8 countries, for example, official (i.e., goverment-established) interest rates ranged from 9 to 24 percent, while rates from traditional (nonofficial) sources ranged from 29 to 240 percent (see Table 2).[49] As a first step, then, official interest-rate limits should be rescinded and

As a first step, official interest-rate limits should be rescinded, and both private and government-operated banks should increase their lending to small-scale farmers and businessmen.

both private and government-operated banks should increase their lending to small-scale farmers and businessmen, the former through loan guarantees and the latter through making more funds available at competitive rates.

Tariffs Tariffs often are lowest for heavy industrial equipment, higher for intermediate goods, and highest for consumer goods (Table 3). Frequently, duties on capital goods or manufacturing raw materials are lowered even further, or waived completely for a time as a stimulus to industrial development. Small firms may qualify for these concessions, but either they are unaware of the opportunity or the application process may be too costly and complicated.

Moreover, many small machines that are important to rural, labor-intensive industry are often classified in the higher duty categories of intermediate or consumer goods. In Sierra Leone, for example, sewing machines imported by small tailoring firms are considered luxury consumer items since most,

Table 2

A Comparison of Official and Nonofficial Rates of Interest, Selected Developing Countries

Country	Nonofficial Rate of Interest (percent)	Official Rate of Interest (percent)
Afghanistan	33	—
Colombia	36–60	24
Gambia, Sudan, Sierra Leone	50–100	10–12
Haiti	40–240	12–15
Korea	35–60	17.5
Thailand	29	9

Source: Chuta and Liedholm, cited in note 44, p. 55.

Table 3
Average Tariff Rates by End-use Groups,
Selected Developing Countries (percent)

Group	Ghana 1966	Pakistan 1965/66	Brazil 1964
Capital goods			
Machinery and equipment	2.05	34	44
Intermediate goods			
Unprocessed capital goods	9.26	46	73
Processed capital goods	6.95–14.85	69	73
Unprocessed consumer goods	9.58	31	73
Processed consumer goods	12.99–21.66	81	73
Consumer durables	25.04	114	104
Consumer nondurables			
Essentials	24	70	82–118
Semi-luxuries	54.80	148	82–118
Luxuries	128	180	82–118

Source: Chuta and Liedholm, cited in note 44, p. 57.

if not all, of the work can be done by hand labor.[50] Finally, a major purpose of the high duties, and sometimes quotas, on intermediate and consumer goods is to prevent them from being imported at prices cheaper than they can be manufactured by the country's protected modern industry. In effect, small businesses and consumers are subsidizing large-scale industry. Therefore, many developing countries need to reorient their tariff structures so that the costs of imported heavy machinery and expensive capital goods are a truer reflection of their relative economic scarcity and not artificially cheapened at the expense of more labor-intensive technology.

Foreign Exchange Rates Many developing countries also "overvalue" their currency to lower the cost of importing modern equipment. That is, they subsidize the price of their own currency to keep it high relative to the dollar. This encourages the purchase of labor-saving equipment. Rarely are small businesses able to take advantage of the favorable foreign exchange rate. Since overvalued rates inevitably lead to a shortage of foreign currency due to its below-market price, foreign exchange (e.g., dollars, marks, yen) must be rationed through import licensing procedures. Small businesses are unable to compete for these licenses for both economic and political reasons (including corruption and bureaucratic inertia).

Overvalued exchange rates have two additional disadvantages for rural development. First, exports, including agricultural produce, are discouraged unless the government takes compensating measures. Second, the ability to import equipment relatively cheaply may encourage multinational firms to set up factories. Economists and political leaders have disagreed fiercely for years about the advantages and disadvantages of multinationals. Simply in terms of migration and urbanization, however, multinationals probably on balance exacerbate the situation because they typically pay high salaries and locate in the largest cities. Like tariff rates on heavy machinery imports, therefore, foreign exchange rates often need realignment (i.e., less overvaluation) to reflect more accurately the relative importance of agricultural development and food production.

Tax Laws Tax laws often encourage the growth of modern industry by permitting a reduced rate on machines for a specified number of years or an accelerated depreciation of equipment. Very few small firms qualify because their investment may not be large enough, they may not have a certain number of employees, or the application process

Many developing countries "overvalue" their currency to lower the cost of importing modern equipment.

may be too complicated and time consuming. Indirect taxes, such as sales and excise taxes collected at each stage of the production process, do not affect large integrated companies that own the sources of raw materials as much as small businesses that have to purchase primary and intermediate goods to make their products.

The dominant position often held by large urban industries, therefore, permits them to influence government to use tax and trade policies against potential competitors elsewhere in the country. This situation has not been well studied, but two analyses of exchange rates and trade policies in Brazil in the late 1950s and 1960s showed a pattern of discrimination against the development of industry in smaller cities. Researchers at the World Bank concluded that "it would be reasonable to expect such patterns to prevail in other countries . . . ."[51]

The dominant position held by large urban industries permits them to influence government to use tax and trade policies against potential competitors.

Some countries also tax agricultural exports, thereby openly tapping farm profits to pay for industrial development. The effects in the rural areas are to dampen production of cash crops for export and depress farmers' incomes. The former curbs farm employment growth, while the latter widens the gulf between urban and rural earnings.

The various policies described above also put small-scale farmers on a treadmill. The value of their crops relative to manufactured consumer goods has dropped over the years, and, more important, they cannot afford nor do they have the incentive to purchase additional agricultural inputs to expand their output. For the nation as a whole, it is much more expensive to create modern, industrial jobs than employment in rural areas, even though industrial workers are generally more productive. In addition, workers in the modern sector, who are often unionized, continuously exert political pressure for higher wages and greater fringe benefits.

The urban bias, which makes it easier to import capital-intensive equipment, in the end slows employment growth.

53

As a result, private employers have an ongoing incentive to purchase machinery rather than hire more labor when they expand production. Thus, the urban bias, which makes it easier to import capital-intensive equipment, in the end slows employment growth.

Small-Farm Agricultural Development

The disincentives to agricultural growth are no longer simply unfortunate. They are leading many peoples and regions in developing countries to the verge of starvation. Countries that do not grow enough food to feed themselves must increase production by 3.4 percent a year just maintain by 1990 the inadequate per capita consumption levels of 1975.[52] However, present trends indicate they will be able to boost production by only 2.7 percent a year, with only the handful of oil exporters able to afford large imports of food. Table 4 illustrates the

Table 4
Food Deficits in Selected Developing Countries, 1975 and 1990 (projected)

Country	Actual 1975		Projected 1990	
	Deficit (in million metric tons)	Percent of Consumption	Deficit (in million metric tons)	Percent of Consumption
Bangladesh	1.0	7	6.4–8.0	30–35
Bolivia and Haiti	0.3	24	0.7–0.8	35–38
Burma	0.4[a]	7[a]	1.9–2.4	21–25
Egypt	3.7	35	4.9	32
Ethiopia	0.1	2	2.1–2.3	26–28
India	1.4	1	17.6–21.9	10–12
Indonesia	2.1	8	6.0–7.7	14–17
Nigeria	0.4	2	17.1–20.5	35–39
Philippines	0.3	4	1.4–1.7	11–13
Sahel Group	0.4	9	3.2–3.5	44–46

[a]Surplus
Source: "Food needs of developing countries," cited in note 36, p.18.

projected increases in food deficits between 1975 and 1990 for a number of developing countries. The trend can change if unused land is cultivated, yields are increased significantly by using more irrigation and fertilizers, and small farmers with labor-intensive methods are given help and encouragement.

In Argentina, Brazil, and Chile, it is estimated that small farmers produce twice the value of produce per unit of cultivated land as large farmers. It has been further estimated that, if the larger farms of Brazil, Colombia, India, Malaysia, Pakistan, and the Philippines were broken up, total output would increase between 19 percent (in India) and 49 percent (in Pakistan).[53] Small farmers tend to be more productive because they use more labor, plant more per hectare, and double-crop more often. Plantation owners in Latin America routinely leave large sections fallow. Even though some of these highly mechanized farms produce more per hectare than small farms when fully cultivated, their real unit costs of production may still be higher because of the relatively high purchase and maintenance costs of their capital equipment. Table 5 provides illustrative data on small- versus large-farm productivity for 12 developing countries.

The enhancement of the small farmer advocated here is different from the agricultural development programs tried in some countries during the past two decades. These programs emphasized the use of modern technology to increase production, and favored large landowners because only they could afford the new machines, seeds, fertilizers, and the risks associated with a new technology. Many governments reduced interest rates or provided other subsidies to farmers to encourage the purchase of tractors. In Pakistan, for example, tractors cost only about half as much as in the United States.[54]

The disincentives to agricultural growth are no longer simply unfortunate. They are leading many peoples and regions to the verge of starvation.

Small farmers tend to be more productive because they use more labor, plant more per hectare, and double-crop more often.

55

Table 5

Output per Hectare on Small and Large Farms: Selected Developing Countries, 1970 (million kilocalorie equivalent)[a]

Country	Farms below 5 Hectares	Farms above 20 Hectares
Brazil	5.9	4.2
Colombia	7.0	3.7
Ghana	5.8	5.6
India	6.1	3.4
Iraq	10.6	2.0
Jamaica	8.0	28.0
Korea, Republic of	13.7	—
Liberia	7.8	3.7
Malawi	6.0	—
Pakistan	6.6	4.1
Peru	3.9	11.0
Uruguay	3.5	4.5

[a]Nonfood products converted on the basis of equivalent value in wheat.
Source: Eckholm, cited in note 53, p.17.

There are many questions on how to apply the small-farm approach since few projects have been fully evaluated. But there is enough evidence for some tentative conclusions:[55]

- Small farmers can be agents of change if they participate in the design of well-planned, carefully implemented projects.

- Projects that reach large numbers of farmers are not excessively costly. In many successful projects, the capital cost per beneficiary has been low.

- Small-farm projects can be as productive and economically attractive as more conventional ones benefiting far fewer people.

- Development can be much more rapid than is sometimes believed, and well-planned programs with incentives for small farmers can produce dramatic income increases beyond subsistence levels.

- Interest in labor-intensive agriculture is growing among leaders of developing countries.

There have been three very broad stages in the evolution of agriculture: subsistence, mixed, and specialized farming. Much of the developing world is still at the first stage, with few countries engaged in mixed farming and even fewer in specialized agriculture. The urgent need for more food requires far greater production than is possible at the subsistence level. But countries with unemployment problems may not wish to encourage specialized agriculture because it is very capital intensive, the extreme example being the highly mechanized agribusiness farms of the United States.

Subsistence-level farming persists because farmers cannot afford either the seeds and equipment to plant cash crops or the risk that harvests may fail or prices drop. A number of programs could help with such problems, including price supports, credit programs, extension services, and technological and biological research. A key program is land reform and, as discussed below, the political difficulties of changing ownership patterns places this among the most important long-term policies.

A number of programs could help subsistence-level farmers, including price supports, credit programs, extension services, and technological and biological research.

In the drive to industrialize, many countries adopted cheap-food policies by purchasing crops at relatively low prices or setting ceilings on the prices farmers could receive. They believed lower food prices would leave consumers with more money for the purchase of manufactured goods. A number of studies have concluded, however, that small farmers cannot earn a profit without higher price supports. Small farmers cannot purchase fertilizers, water pumps, or seeds if they have no reasonable hope of earning more than their costs. Although

57

higher price supports may raise the cost of food beyond the reach of some poor workers in urban areas, goverments can alleviate this problem through consumption subsidies of basic staples. Farm employment and incomes, however, can be expected to rise quickly with rising cash crop prices. Larger farmers might hire more help. Sharecroppers' income could be expected to rise. Rural artisans could expect more business. Moneylenders and richer farmers might compete to make loans as their cash incomes rose, thereby reducing interest rates for smaller farmers. There is every reason to believe that, within a short time, the benefits of higher crop prices would ripple advantageously through the rural economy.

In most cases, it will also be necessary to extend credit to small farmers for the purchase of additional seed, fertilizer, and simple equipment needed to increase production. A number of countries have programs to extend credit to groups rather than individuals, a policy that seems to reduce risks to both borrower and lender. Such integrated credit programs have led to product gains in many countries.[56] Generally the programs operate in a few areas of a country, although several have been extended nationwide.

Small farmers in well-run credit and extension programs are more likely to adopt new techniques and produce higher yields than large farmers.

Small farmers using traditional methods also need instruction and advice about new seeds and techniques. Preliminary surveys indicate that small farmers in well-run credit and extension programs are more likely to adopt new techniques and produce higher yields than large farmers.[57]

Ultimately, increased production will be of no value if the farmer does not know where, when, and at what price to best sell his produce. This knowledge is extremely important because all progress depends on farmers selling their crops at a profit. A number of countries offer some kind of marketing service.[58]

Special Problems of Women

Women tend to be heavily involved in agriculture in regions where techniques are very simple and involve much manual labor. In Africa, where much of the farming is still done using traditional techniques, most of the work is performed by women. Men and women share the work in Asia, where the populations are dense and the farming techniques require intensive labor. In the Near East, however, women's status is very low, partly, perhaps, because ploughs are used and agriculture is predominantly a male occupation. In all areas, however, women have had to take over on many small farms as males continue to migrate to the cities. Very broadly, then, women comprise 60 to 80 percent of the agricultural labor force in Africa, about 50 percent in Asia, 40 percent in Latin America, and a minor proportion in the Near East.[59] Almost all of this labor is unpaid because it is done on family farms.

Only recently has it become clear that more women are migrating to the cities, both married ones moving with their husbands and unmarried ones. The trend has been particularly strong in Latin America, where women often comprise a majority of the urban population. The two sexes are about equal in number in the cities of East Asia, while men still predominate in the urban centers of the rest of the developing world, but less so with each year.[60]

Some of the reasons women migrate are identical with those of men: land has been lost to moneylenders; women expect to earn more in the cities than in the countryside; mechanization has made their labor superfluous. But there are other reasons that arise out of the traditional roles of wife and mother. The most eligible and the greatest number of unmarried men are in the largest cities of most countries. Women who have been able to take advantage of increasing educational opportunities are particularly likely to migrate in search of a husband.

Women have had to take over on many small farms as males continue to migrate to the cities. Almost all of this labor is unpaid because it is done on family farms.

Some of the reasons women migrate are identical with those of men: land has been lost to moneylenders; women expect to earn more in the cities than in the countryside; mechanization has made their labor superfluous.

59

These women, in turn, have become more employable, which makes them sought after as brides.

The number of women opting for a better life away from the poverty of rural existence can be expected to grow as educational and job barriers are removed. In addition, impoverished families may send daughters to the cities not so much to marry (although marriage is always a consideration) as to get a job and send money home. Generally, such women wind up in service rather than industrial work—as domestics in Latin America, for example.

As societies modernize, then, women can be expected to migrate to urban centers in increasing numbers if employment does not grow in rural areas or if single men leave in significant numbers. Therefore, employment and equity policies should seek to slow the migration of both men and women. It may be necessary to target programs to ensure that they reach women in those areas where they do much of the agricultural work. Credit usually has not been extended to women because the land that is used as collateral is held in a man's name or is owned communally. When it has, studies indicate that the repayment record of women is often better than that of male farmers.

Furthermore, it is hard to imagine how production can be increased where women are the important workers if they are not brought into the agricultural decision-making process. Programs for production growth, which is stimulated by technological development, should be "female conscious" because standard mechanization has almost always led to the displacement of women.

Even something as potentially important as land reform must be examined for its effects on women. In a reform program, land titles almost always are given to males, which may drastically change the normal pattern of communal ownership and lower the status of women. This has happened in parts of Africa. In some cases, women could no longer farm or take part in the work of cooperatives or other decision-making bodies.[61]

Education and Health

In the 1970s almost 80 percent of the population in the 25 least developed countries was illiterate. This condition was much more common in rural than urban areas and far more prevalent among women than men because of traditional biases.[62] The usual prescription for illiteracy and lack of social mobility is education, but the formal school systems of the 1950s and 1960s did little to alleviate unemployment, poverty, inequality, and rural stagnation. Schooling systems patterned after those in the West or the Soviet Union taught little that was relevant to rural life or any of the professions socially and economically vital to development, such as engineering and agronomy. With a general education, students felt they were entitled to white-collar employment or to be trained as skilled workers. But the opportunities did not grow as rapidly as the number of students. As the number of educated unemployed and underemployed increased in various developing countries, young people strove for even more inappropriate education in a desperate attempt to overqualify for the modern sector jobs.[63]

Attempts to change the system, to make it less elitist and more relevant to rural life and work, have been resisted by parents because they realize that reform would make their children less competitive in the urban employment market. Parents make the perfectly valid point that economic incentives should change along with educational values. Governments could eliminate educational standards where none are needed to perform successfully at a job or set reasonable ones where such standards are

In the 1970s almost 80 percent of the population in the 25 least developed countries was illiterate. This condition was much more common in rural than urban areas and far more prevalent among women than men because of traditional biases.

Efforts should be made to hold down the supply of urban job applicants by redirecting training toward areas of employment scarcity.

relevant. If there are more qualified applicants than available positions, which is almost certain to be the case, efforts should be made to hold down the supply by redirecting training toward areas of employment scarcity.

Revised curricula, adult education, agricultural and vocational instruction, and leadership training programs are some of the specific reforms being tried in various countries. Benin, Upper Volta, Mali, Nigeria, Senegal, Kenya, and Peru have moved (cautiously) from academic training in rural schools to curricula designed to prepare youths for rural employment.[64] Educational assistants are used to reach larger numbers of pupils in Indonesia, the Philippines, Benin, and Upper Volta. Higher schooling is being made available in regional centers or by mobile units in Bolivia, Colombia, Bangladesh, El Salvador, and Mexico.

Numerous countries have various kinds of programs to teach local leaders management, supervision, and planning skills.[65] Often, local participation and leadership training are organized through multipurpose cooperatives, as in Bangladesh, Bolivia, Ecuador, Guatemala, India, Kenya, Paraguay, the Philippines, Taiwan, Tanzania, Thailand, Uganda, and Venezuela.

Like the better schools and jobs, the best health and sanitation services can be found in the cities. Large hospitals staffed by qualified doctors and nurses with modern equipment can usually be found only in the capital cities. Nothing remotely comparable exists in rural areas. But there is an additional problem. Large hospitals staffed by Western-trained doctors use modern, high-technology equipment that is inappropriate and mostly irrelevant for the needs of rural areas, where preventive public health measures are more urgently required than curative services. To provide rural preventive health care, "barefoot" doctor programs using paramed-

Large hospitals staffed by Western-trained doctors use modern, high-technology equipment that is inappropriate and mostly irrelevant for the needs of rural areas.

62

ics, midwives, and nurses to staff clinics or mobile units are being tried in some countries, including Bolivia, Cameroon, Colombia, Malaysia, Thailand, and Venezuela.[66] Visiting paramedics are particularly important among cultures that do not permit women to travel far from home.

The immediate effect of better rural health care may be to reduce mortality, and hence to increase population pressures. But, in time, reduced mortality is an important factor encouraging parents to have smaller families because they feel confident that the children they have will survive.

Government Decentralization

The civil service structure in most developing countries also exhibits an excessive urban bias. The prized positions—those that pay well and lead to promotions—are almost always located in the capital city. But many of the real needs are in rural areas, and it is difficult if not impossible to plan and implement rural development programs from distant urban locations. Consequently, a government committed to rural development as a means of alleviating problems of rapid urbanization needs to demonstrate its commitment through the decentralization of its most talented civil servants. A rural-oriented bureaucracy would be a very visible sign to farmers and artisans that the government was determined to help them, and, therefore, could be trusted. Specific steps could include:

- Extra pay for service in rural areas.

- Assigning the best civil service entrants to rural areas.

- Making promotions dependent on performance in the field rather than on qualifying examinations.

- Coordinating services, particularly agricultural

The civil service structure in most developing countries exhibits an excessive urban bias. A rural-oriented bureaucracy would indicate to farmers and artisans that the government was determined to help them.

and business, by giving authority to an officer in the locality, rather than to a ministry office in the capital.

- Creating a special staff, perhaps in the office of the president or prime minister, to monitor plans for agricultural development.

- Reassigning many experts from the central banks, planning commissions, and nationalized industries to evaluation teams that would help local officials prepare and monitor agricultural and dispersed industrial projects.

- Longer job postings in a particular town.

- Freezing or reducing the benefits of urban assignments, such as allowances for higher costs of living.

Long-Term Policies

In addition to the aforementioned areas of policy designed to promote a more equitable balance between rural and urban economic and social opportunities in the short run, there are a number of critical long-run policy strategies that most developing-country governments need to consider. Chief among these are programs of dispersed urbanization, appropriate technology development, new colonization, land reform, and the gradual elimination of urban wage biases. Each is briefly discussed below.

Dispersed Urbanization

Development programs designed to geographically disperse the urban growth pattern can be very popular with politicians because they bring construction, jobs, and income to their areas. The programs try to stimulate the growth of a mix of industries outside the major cities by focusing new investment in regional towns. Most programs of dispersed urbanization have two goals. First, they help to redirect migration streams from a country's metropolitan centers to the cities and small towns of each region. Second, they help to keep residents from moving out of their region. A number of countries have initiated such programs,[67] but many more exist only on paper in development plans.

All too often, programs of dispersed urbanization become confused with the theory of "growth poles" that sometimes dominates the practice of regional development. The basic idea of growth poles is to choose one or more cities in a predominantly rural region for intensive investment. The objective is to hold those industries that can be linked to the hinterland in order to create a more integrated regional economy. Many past efforts at creating regional growth poles were costly and short-lived because they involved grand, often nationwide, plans. Sometimes, the plans overlooked the very kinds of industry that make regional development worth undertaking—those using relatively large amounts of labor. For example, Mexico, India, and Pakistan convinced some companies in the 1960s to leave the large cities, but it was big plants using even less labor than the average for industry as a whole that relocated in smaller towns.[68]

Consequently, programs of dispersed urbanization can be most effective where public and private investment is focused on the establishment and/or expansion of selected, labor-intensive industries located in small and medium-sized towns as well as in larger regional cities. Mexico and India, for example, revised their earlier programs and by the 1970s they, Thailand, Peru, Malaysia, Taiwan, the Philippines, Puerto Rico, Swaziland, Nigeria, Israel, and Turkey were promoting decentralization of labor-intensive industries. Of these, Taiwan, Israel,

Critical long-term strategies are programs of dispersed urbanization, appropriate technology development, new colonization, land reform, and the gradual elimination of urban-wage biases.

Programs of dispersed urbanization can be most effective where public and private investment is focused on labor-intensive industries located in small and medium-sized towns.

and Puerto Rico have been most successful because they coordinated the industrial decentralization process with the construction of needed rural infrastructure.

Incentives to relocate, such as favorable tax treatment and subsidized interest rates, have not been very effective. Where they have led to plant movings, the incentives have also at times stimulated the purchase of more capital-intensive equipment sooner than might otherwise have been the case.[69]

The most popular inducements in many countries were industrial estates.[70] In India, for example, 340 estates were built between 1955 and 1970. Typically, utilities, credit, training, trading, and advisory services were made available to businesses locating in the estates. However, not enough businesses moved to justify the high costs of estates. Similarly, new towns have rarely attracted much industry unless they were built close enough to the largest cities to become their satellites.[71]

It may be that most relocation programs will not be as successful as assistance to existing enterprises to expand and to new ones to begin. Relocation may be uneconomical in most cases because the plants in the big cities use relatively little labor. There is not much reason for them to move, nor for government to waste its scarce resources trying to induce them. Size is not the issue; the amount of productive employment is. For example, the bulk processing, transporting, and marketing of some crops for urban and foreign markets can be done most economically by firms using labor-intensive methods. Such enterprises belong in rural centers.

Small and medium-sized enterprises are much more likely to use labor-intensive processes than large ones. They are also much more in need of government help in obtaining credit and information. Small businesses depend most heavily on

Government may have to be the prime lender where enterprises are small and scattered, which is usually the case in regions devoted to subsistence-level farming.

family savings to establish themselves, and on reinvested profits to expand. They may borrow from such traditional sources as moneylenders, but, as noted earlier, banks, credit unions, and cooperatives often believe that loans to small firms are risky and costly to service. Therefore, government may have to be the prime lender where enterprises are small and scattered, which is usually the case in regions devoted to subsistence-level farming. A rural extension service for nonfarm enterprises could, among its other services, evaluate applicants and supervise loans. In the larger towns and small cities, credit unions and cooperatives may be willing to extend credit if the government would provide guarantees against default.

Political pressures and a desire to launch a strong program may tempt governments to subsidize interest rates to small enterprises to a greater extent than is necessary. However, this could conflict with other goals. Businesses would have an incentive to purchase too much labor-saving machinery if funds at artificially low interest rates were readily available. Besides, they are accustomed to paying market or "black market" rates for credit. Therefore, it is likely that the amount they could borrow would be of as much concern to them as the interest rate they have to pay. Very low rates may thus be both unnecessary and counterproductive.

Regional development banks could play a crucial role in providing both financial and managerial expertise to small-town industries.

An industrial extension service could also deliver technical assistance. Programs in Kenya, Ghana, and India have done so, but there is no good evaluation of the results.[72] There are some suggestions that extension services have not been as effective as vocational training programs and apprenticeship systems in introducing and upgrading skills of business owners and workers.[73]

Effective extension services could provide management assistance. Apparently, most businesses are not aware that they need help in evaluating costs, making inventory plans, adjusting production processes to utilize local resources, and the like.[74] Regional development banks in particular could play a crucial role in providing both financial and managerial expertise to small-town industries.

Developing Appropriate Technology

Industry   Steel and fertilizers, to mention just two important products, are made most cheaply by using the very latest Western technology. The Chinese found this out during the disastrous Great Leap Forward in the early 1960s when they tried to produce steel in towns and villages. But where this is not true—with nondurable consumer products, construction, and the processing of agricultural goods, for example—there is still very little modern, labor-intensive technology available. In the early 1970s, therefore, interest began to focus in several Western and developing countries on the need for expanded research and development related to appropriate technology. Much more needs to be done. Not only must more technology research be created and fostered in the developing countries, but there should also be closer contact with regional entrepreneurs and government development officials to ensure that the technology developed is needed and can be used efficiently. Western scientists and institutions can be expected to continue to help train researchers in the developing world and to carry out some of the research and development. The only question is: will this training and research continue to focus on labor-saving technologies or will it begin to seriously explore the possibilities of more appropriate capital- and energy-saving techniques?[75]

New products and techniques may require training to develop new skills. Much of the traditional work in carpentry, metalworking, and tailoring is changing because of more modern needs and styles. New skills such as baking and furniture making are wanted in some areas. Many countries have responded by creating a system of vocational training that also covers traditional skills. The costs, however, have generally been high.[76] It would seem wisest to work more closely within the traditional apprenticeship system. It has trained numerous workers, many of whom become entrepreneurs. Vocational training could limit itself to doing what the apprenticeship system cannot or will not do in a particular area. In that case, a mixture of permanent and mobile centers and self-help schemes, wherein government provides instruction and equipment and the local community provides buildings and materials, may reduce the high cost of training programs.

Agriculture There are two technological methods of increasing crop yields. Mechanization too often displaces labor without reducing per unit costs of production. On the other hand, biological (hybrid seeds) and chemical (fertilizers, insecticides) methods most often increase output per worker, which provides an incentive to hire more laborers.

Mechanization too often displaces labor without reducing per unit costs of agricultural production. On the other hand, biological and chemical methods most often increase output per worker, which provides an incentive to hire more laborers.

An analysis in 1978 of 30 studies of the use of tractors in southern Asia found that they did not increase cropping intensities, yields, or gross returns per hectare. On the other hand, irrigation and new seeds significantly increased yields. The review " . . . largely supports the view that tractors are a substitute for labor and bullock power, which implies that, at existing and projected human and animal hiring rates, tractors fail to be a strong engine of economic growth."[77] In some cases, even bullocks are uneconomical. If they are privately owned on small farms, they become almost a fixed cost that cannot be used to full capacity.[78]

In some instances small tractors can be very useful. They can remove seasonal bottlenecks so that more land may be farmed. Similarly, soil that is hard to work using traditional methods might be cropped a number of times a year. Selective mechanization programs have increased employment and output in Gambia, Ivory Coast, Japan, Kenya, Malaysia, Mali, Morocco, the Philippines, Taiwan, and Uganda.[79]

Proponents of rural development began in the early 1970s to emphasize the need to adapt technology for use by small farmers. Experience had shown that peasants adopted new technology only when it was proven that it was not very risky, and did not need sophisticated management skills.[80] Innovative technology from the West, even that of the Green Revolution, would not meet these criteria without modification.

Not a great deal has been done, however, although Bangladesh, Gambia, Pakistan, Taiwan, and Tanzania have small-scale implements programs to reduce drudgery and increase productivity.[81] Taiwan, the Philippines, and India train farmers in the use of labor rather than machines for the more careful soil preparation, weeding, and fertilizer application necessary in fields with new, higher yield seeds. The relative inactivity may lie in the very nature of agricultural research: foreign scientists have long dominated the field, and much of the research is basic, with applicable results coming only after many years of work. There is an important and continuing role for developed-country scientists, private institutions, and governments, but it must begin to focus on the immediate needs of small-scale farmers.[82]

Although the basic aim of fostering a technology that will help peasants increase production is the same for Africa, Asia, and Latin America, the research emphasis in Africa must be on small and very basic improvements in implements, soil conservation, and seeds because hand methods and shifting cultivation are still prevalent. Somewhat

Developed-country scientists, institutions, and governments have an important role in developing countries, but they must begin to focus on the immediate needs of small-scale farmers.

70

more sophisticated technology is needed in Latin America. In Asia, irrigation, drainage, fertilizer, and multiple cropping technology has to be developed to compensate for the lack of land.

Equally important as technology is the training of agricultural experts. Surveys have revealed that in perhaps only three nations—Liberia, Egypt, and Honduras—did more than 10 percent of college graduates have agricultural degrees. In another seven countries, fewer than 3 percent of college graduates had agricultural degrees. Many countries had no graduates with such degrees.[83]

This enormous lack of people able to develop, adapt, and apply research could be more serious than a lack of funds. The major cause of failure of farm water projects, for example, lies in inadequate government planning, organization, and management of irrigation systems.[84]

Colonization

Many countries have thought they could significantly reduce urban and rural unemployment, increase agricultural output, and promote a more equitable distribution of income by opening up new lands to settlement.

The Paraguayan case is important not simply because colonization worked, but also because it dramatically confirms the bits and pieces of evidence that creating employment opportunities in rural areas is one viable option to unbridled urbanization.

Although the focus of colonization is on agriculture, the growth of towns to serve as centers for farmers' markets and small and medium enterprises is also envisaged. The results have generally been disappointing. Costs have been higher than expected, not enough settlers come, and life is often difficult for those who do.[85] Failure may result from lack of infrastructure, the wrong kinds of people moving in, difficulty in using the old farming methods on a different kind of land, and a number of other reasons.

One notable exception seems to be Paraguay.[86] A land settlement program began there in 1962, with peasants moving from the center of the country toward the north and east. The government provided few services for the colonists, and in the end they may not have been much better off than previously. Yet the migration was significant enough to enable Paraguay to escape the overurbanization rampant throughout the developing world.

The Paraguayan case is important not simply because colonization worked, but also because it dramatically confirms the bits and pieces of evidence that creating employment opportunities in rural areas "is one viable option to unbridled urbanization."[87]

Land Reform

Without widespread and lasting land reform, the future is grim for the approximately 600 million landless laborers, tenants, and owners of marginal-sized plots. Many are born into debt and die in debt, with the time in between a never-ceasing struggle to survive. Up to half of their children do not live to age five. In Bangladesh during the food shortages of 1975, for example, the death rate of groups with fewer than two hectares of land was triple that of peasants with three or more hectares.[88]

The numbers of landless laborers and small landowners have increased, and today they are a majority in the rural areas of most of Asia and Latin America.[89] Their proportion in Asia ranges from 53 percent in India to 85 percent in Java, while in Latin America it ranges from 55 percent in Costa Rica to 85 percent in Bolivia and Guatemala. There are no good data for Africa, but the indications are that the proportion, though much smaller, is rapidly growing.

Several land redistribution programs have worked well, mainly because the new farmers were given credit, advice, and other technical supports along with title to their land. Programs in the 1960s and early 1970s in parts of Bolivia, Chile, Venezuela, Indonesia, Thailand, Kenya, Benin, Sudan, Tanzania, and Egypt raised incomes and, in many cases, productivity.[90] Reform programs in Argentina, Bangladesh, Brazil, Colombia, Ecuador, Guatemala, India, Indonesia, Iraq, Ivory Coast, Pakistan, Peru, the Philippines, and Turkey were less successful as new farmers received little or no support.

The most widespread and lasting reforms since World War II took place in Japan, South Korea, and Taiwan despite the lack of excess land, a situation typical throughout Asia. They are now nations of peasant landowners whose yields are much higher than ever before. Reform was pushed through in the aftermath of war or because of the fear of revolution, leading some observers to argue that meaningful reform can only occur as a result of crisis.[91]

In some cases, reforms short of land redistribution, such as rent ceilings for tenants, assurances that they have the right to continue to farm the land, or clearing titles to plots where ownership is in doubt, would also lead to higher incomes and productivity. The enhanced security felt by tenants after such reforms in Sri Lanka, Taiwan, Ecuador, and parts of the Philippines led them to adopt new production techniques.

The great problem remains the powerful opposition of the wealthy. One interesting suggestion on how to mobilize political support for reform has been offered by Michael Lipton.[92] He argues that almost everyone in the rural economy—moneylenders, rich farmers, small farmers, landless laborers—is harmed by urban biases that generally keep the price of necessary materials high. If land is so grossly maldistributed that only large plantation owners would be affected adversely by reform, the rest of the rural elite might be willing to combine

Several land redistribution programs have worked well, mainly because the new farmers were given credit, advice, and other technical supports along with title to their land.

If land is so grossly maldistributed that only large plantation owners would be adversely affected by reform, the rest of the rural elite might be willing to combine forces with peasants and the landless in a broad program of reapportionment.

73

forces with peasants and the landless in a broad program of ridding themselves of the urban bias and reapportioning land. Recent developments in Nicaragua provide one illustration of this kind of coalition. The initial benefits of reform might go disproportionately to the well-off, but the poorer people would still stand a better chance of obtaining more than they ever had. The grossest inequities in land holdings exist in Latin America; in 1975, for example, 7 percent of the farms contained 93 percent of the arable land.[93]

Subtle pressures for land reform from international organizations and governments are important and continuing. The United Nations, for example, holds conferences on agrarian reform, and many of its publications stress its importance and discuss its implications. The World Bank announced in 1975 that it would generally not fund projects whose benefits would go disproportionately to the wealthy. In 1978, the United States announced it would give technical and financial assistance to reform programs and would consider withholding aid from projects that harmed the poor.[94] Such efforts must be subtle and tentative lest donor governments and agencies begin to feel they have the right to intervene in the internal affairs of other countries. It may also be that if developing nations redirect their energies from heavy industry to agriculture and small-scale manufacturing, governments will sense the need to institute land reform in order to raise production.

Eliminating Urban-Wage Biases

Government and private modern sector urban salaries at all occupational levels are relatively high. Moreover, in many cases these well-paid jobs are also very secure. One reason is that workers in the largest industries often are well organized. Another is that many governments legislate minimum-wage levels to protect workers against exploitation and to provide some security in an economy burdened with mass unemployment. As the minimum is periodically adjusted upward, the entire wage scale tends to rise, often disproportionately.

Government employees and unions use their political and economic power to raise wages, which may lessen the opportunities available for nonorganized job seekers. Moreover, employees of large plantations are often adversely affected by such measures because it is usually impossible to enforce a minimum wage among the farms and enterprises in rural areas. Thus, when minimum wages rose by 20 percent in Nigeria in 1964, employment dropped on large farms because it became cheaper to use machines.[95]

Results are similar in the cities. Union scales and minimum wages, in combination with favorable foreign exchange rates, interest rate subsidies, and tax waivers, lead heavy industry to import labor-saving machines. Managers would behave irrationally if they did not take advantage of such incentives. Workers and unions also have no reason to complain as long as they have the power to prevent layoffs. In that case, currently employed workers retain their jobs at higher salaries. At times, unions benefit further because a few new jobs are created. However, the nation as a whole loses because employment expands at a slower rate than would be true if incentives for efficient, labor-intensive methods of production existed.

A number of corrective measures may be taken, all of which would probably be politically unpopular. In the previous section on short-term policies, we emphasized the need to rid the economy of subsidized capital. The first step, then, is to eliminate the tax breaks, relatively low interest rates, and

Government employees and unions use their political and economic power to raise wages, which may lessen the opportunities available for nonorganized job seekers.

other measures that make it inexpensive to buy machinery. The next step is to prevent the price of labor from becoming artificially high. A freeze on government salaries, as imposed for example in Tanzania, is one method. This may have the important side effect of moderating wage demands in the private sector. Another method is to set the minimum real wage, if there must be one, at or near the average level of agricultural incomes. These wage policies would not only discourage acquisition of capital-intensive equipment, but also reduce the gap between urban and rural incomes. None of the agricultural and rural development schemes mentioned above would significantly reduce urban migration if the artificial economic advantages of the city were not simultaneously eliminated.

National leaders will need courage, political skill, administrative ability, and self-confidence—not the most common combination of human attributes— to enact some of the recommendations for reversing current urbanization trends. This assumes that they would want to, which often, of course, has not been the case because decision makers have simply been the representatives of urban (and rural) elites intent on maintaining their privileges. The national leadership must make a strong commitment to change before there can ever be hope of bringing about geographically balanced and sustained economic growth.

Two groups are likely to oppose some or all of the changes proposed for cities: unions and the urban wealthy class. The unions can be expected to oppose the freezing of private industry and government real wages in the cities, including the minimum rates. Normally, unions are not very large because employment in the modern sector, where almost all their membership exists, is limited. Some observers suggest that wage increases exacerbate inflation, leaving workers no better off than before.[96] Unions and their leaders might be encouraged or persuaded to forego wage increases, or to be satisfied with minor cost-of-living adjustments, if the policies to expand employment resulted in more members and enhanced internal political power. In two countries in which urban wages were frozen, Tanzania and Cuba, unions were forced to work closely with government. But these countries are by no means representative of the developing world.

One interesting suggestion by World Bank economists for dealing with elites and other groups with

The national leadership must make a strong commitment to change before there can ever be hope of bringing about geographically balanced and sustained economic growth.

77

vested interests is to leave their wealth alone but transfer proportionately more of the annual increase in national income to poor groups.[97] This "redistribution from growth," brought about by such means as progressive income taxes, would gradually increase the share of wealth owned by poorer people. Several studies indicate, however, that new income is distributed much as wealth already is; that is, the character of a country's economic and social structure determines how the proceeds of growth are distributed, despite such measures as progressive taxation.[98] Therefore, this counter-argument concludes, there must be redistribution *before* growth, with fundamental reforms such as land redistribution being first steps, not measures that can be delayed until a more propitious time. Clearly, differing circumstances in various countries will dictate alternative policy agendas and timing sequences.

Having listed some formidable obstacles to the thoroughgoing reforms essential to a more balanced and broad-based development, we might be tempted to stop in despair or argue that violent radical change is the only answer. As detailed earlier in this paper, a number of successful attempts at reform were not immediately all-embracing. For those not satisfied with anything less than sweeping change, it does seem that a crisis such as war or revolution is the great catalyst, as was the case in Japan, South Korea, Taiwan, China, and Cuba. A widespread crisis, however, may already be brewing, for, with the exception of some oil producers, South Korea, Taiwan, Brazil, and perhaps Argentina and India, prospects for developing countries in the 1980s appear grim.[99] The food situation in much of Africa and South Asia is precarious and expected to get worse. Energy import costs have greatly exacerbated balance-of-payments and debt service difficulties. In few places has the well-being of the majority of people been significantly im-

One interesting suggestion for dealing with elites and other groups with vested interests is to leave their wealth alone but to transfer proportionately more of the annual increase in national income to poor groups.

proved. In order for that well-being to improve, a viable, broad-based, and self-sustaining rural development effort will be necessary. Primate cities can no longer be permitted to capture a disproportionate share of the economic pie. In fact, it may not be possible for them to continue to do so.

If the countryside does not prosper, the cities will continue to deteriorate. This is the ultimate paradox of the worsening urban crisis in developing countries.

If the countryside does not prosper, the cities will continue to deteriorate. This is the ultimate paradox of the urban crisis in developing countries.

Appendix

Table A-1
Size of Urban Population in Major World Regions
and Selected Countries, 1950–2000 (in thousands)

	1950	1960	1970	1975	1980	1990	2000
World Total	724,147	1,012,084	1,354,357	1,560,860	1,806,809	2,422,293	3,208,028
Developed regions	448,929	572,730	702,876	767,302	834,401	969,226	1,092,470
Developing regions	275,218	439,354	651,481	793,558	972,408	1,453,067	2,115,558
Africa	31,818	49,506	80,373	103,032	132,951	219,202	345,757
Algeria	1948	3287	6529	9024	12,065	19,714	28,021
Egypt	6532	9818	14,080	16,346	19,119	26,604	37,048
Ethiopia	761	1284	2315	3273	4562	8555	15,140
Ghana	727	1575	2511	3193	4104	6830	10,843
Kenya	336	597	1145	1592	2223	4314	8125
Morocco	2345	3412	5236	6551	8265	13,126	19,704
Nigeria	3595	5642	9009	11,449	14,811	25,665	45,041
Senegal	563	704	930	1070	1265	1896	3002
South Africa	5261	7424	10,281	11,934	14,154	20,417	30,109
Sudan	572	1212	2571	3722	5305	10,014	16,551
Zambia	428	742	1290	1704	2235	3802	6260
Latin America	67,511	106,559	162,355	198,366	240,592	343,304	466,234
Argentina	11,205	15,172	18,616	20,436	22,300	25,818	28,875
Brazil	19,064	32,996	53,253	66,621	82,172	119,271	163,027
Chile	3558	5145	7048	8044	9116	11,390	13,460
Colombia	4334	7665	13,209	16,946	21,212	31,102	41,779
Ecuador	911	1490	2384	2971	3707	5735	8564
Guatemala	921	1317	1889	2269	2763	4193	6384
Mexico	11,348	18,458	29,706	37,318	46,660	71,069	102,293
Nicaragua	397	609	930	1163	1457	2256	3396
Paraguay	474	631	853	1003	1205	1800	2708
Peru	2811	4265	7605	9619	11,942	17,498	24,132
Venezuela	2739	5084	8048	9795	11,776	16,364	21,125
Asia	175,618	283,026	407,646	490,570	596,609	885,544	1,297,719
Bangladesh	1786	2649	5150	6838	9531	18,192	32,095
India	59,247	76,575	106,994	127,177	154,524	235,837	360,688
Indonesia	9362	13,522	20,395	25,079	31,293	49,477	76,612
Iran	4087	7249	11,601	14,959	19,209	30,162	43,138
Iraq	1819	2937	5461	7272	9414	14,525	20,366
Nepal	183	285	440	550	708	1245	2275
Philippines	5695	8350	12,387	15,244	18,902	29,198	43,988
South Korea	4347	6843	12,766	16,682	20,921	29,915	37,807
Sri Lanka	1106	1772	2736	3359	4108	6090	8660
Syria	1071	1677	2708	3393	4290	6776	10,105
Turkey	4441	8181	13,536	17,106	21,482	32,684	45,482

Source: United Nations, cited in footnote 8, Table 4 and Annex II, Table 48.

Table A-2
Percent of Population Living in Urban Areas
in Major World Regions and Selected Countries, 1950–2000

	1950	1960	1970	1975	1980	1990	2000
World Total	28.95	33.89	37.51	39.34	41.31	45.88	51.29
Developed regions	52.54	58.73	64.68	67.49	70.15	74.87	78.75
Developing regions	16.71	21.85	25.82	28.03	30.53	36.46	43.46
Africa	14.5	18.2	22.9	25.7	28.9	35.7	42.5
Algeria	22.2	30.4	45.6	53.7	60.9	71.1	76.4
Egypt	31.9	37.9	42.3	43.5	45.4	50.5	57.4
Ethiopia	4.6	6.4	9.3	11.7	14.5	21.0	28.2
Ghana	14.5	23.2	29.1	32.3	35.9	43.5	51.2
Kenya	5.6	7.4	10.2	12.0	14.2	19.5	26.2
Morocco	26.2	29.3	34.6	37.4	40.6	47.5	54.9
Nigeria	10.5	13.1	16.4	18.2	20.4	26.1	33.4
Senegal	21.7	22.6	23.7	24.2	25.4	29.6	36.7
South Africa	42.2	46.6	47.8	48.4	49.6	53.9	60.3
Sudan	6.3	10.3	16.4	20.4	24.8	34.0	42.5
Zambia	17.4	23.1	30.0	33.9	38.0	46.4	54.1
Latin America	41.2	49.6	57.4	61.2	64.7	70.7	75.2
Argentina	65.3	73.6	78.4	80.5	82.4	85.5	87.9
Brazil	36.0	46.1	55.9	60.7	65.0	72.0	76.7
Chile	58.4	67.8	75.2	78.4	81.1	85.1	87.7
Colombia	37.1	48.2	59.8	65.5	70.2	77.1	81.2
Ecuador	28.3	34.4	39.5	41.9	44.7	51.0	58.0
Guatemala	30.5	33.0	35.7	37.0	38.9	44.3	51.6
Mexico	42.7	50.8	59.0	63.0	66.7	72.8	77.4
Nicaragua	35.8	41.4	47.2	50.2	53.3	59.7	65.9
Paraguay	34.6	35.6	37.1	37.9	39.4	44.2	51.4
Peru	35.5	46.3	57.4	63.8	67.4	74.5	79.0
Venezuela	43.2	66.6	74.2	80.2	83.3	87.5	89.7
Asia	16.2	21.2	24.2	26.0	27.9	33.0	40.0
Bangladesh	4.4	5.2	7.6	9.3	11.2	16.1	22.2
India	16.8	17.9	19.7	20.7	22.3	26.9	34.1
Indonesia	12.4	14.6	17.1	18.4	20.2	25.2	32.3
Iran	27.7	33.6	40.9	45.4	49.9	58.1	64.8
Iraq	35.1	42.9	58.4	65.9	71.6	79.5	82.3
Nepal	2.3	3.1	3.9	4.4	5.0	6.8	9.8
Philippines	27.1	30.3	32.9	34.3	36.2	41.6	49.0
South Korea	21.4	27.7	40.7	48.1	54.8	65.2	71.4
Sri Lanka	14.4	17.4	21.9	24.0	26.6	32.9	40.9
Syria	30.6	36.8	43.4	46.7	50.3	57.3	63.9
Turkey	21.3	29.7	38.4	42.9	47.4	55.7	62.7

Source: United Nations, cited in footnote 8, Table 8 and Annex II, Table 50.

1. For an analysis of poverty trends in developing countries, see International Bank for Reconstruction and Development, *World Development Report 1980* (Washington, D.C.: IBRD, 1980), Chapter 4.

2. United Nations, *Concise Report on the World Population Situation in 1977* (New York: United Nations, 1979), ST/ESA/SER.A/63., p. 94.

3. Although these same statements could be made about rural areas—i.e., considerable unemployment, rapid population growth, and inadequate services—the fundamental point is that whereas the basic cause of these rural problems is economic neglect, absolute poverty, and rapid population growth (with causality implied), in urban areas rapid population growth and high unemployment have been *exacerbated* by government policies that created socially uneconomic, artificial incentives for rural youth to leave farms and small towns in search of modern wage employment.

4. For an extensive description and analysis of the nature and degree of urban bias in the development policies of a wide range of developing-world countries, see Michael Lipton, *Why Poor People Stay Poor: Urban Bias in World Development* (Cambridge: Harvard University Press, 1977).

5. International Bank for Reconstruction and Development, *World Bank Operations: Sectoral Programs and Policies* (Washington, D.C.: IBRD, 1972), p. 295.

6. Charles B. Keely, *U.S. Immigration: A Policy Analysis* (New York: The Population Council, 1979).

7. E. F. Szcepanik, "Agricultural capital formation in selected developing countries," Agricultural Planning Studies, no. 11, Food and Agricultural Organization, Rome, 1970, p. 44.

8. For detailed evidence, see Sally Findley, *Planning for Internal Migration: A Review of Issues and Policies for Developing Countries* (Washington, D.C.: 1977), ISP-RD-4, pp. 34–38. See also, United Nations, *Patterns of Urban and*

Rural Population Growth, Population Studies No. 68, Department of Economic and Social Affairs (New York: United Nations, 1980), ST/ESA/ Series A. 68, Chs. 3 and 4.

9. For a mathematical analysis of the mechanism through which rural-to-urban migration and urban natural increase interact in rapidly urbanizing countries, see Nathan Keyfitz, "Do cities grow by natural increase or by migration?," *Geographical Analysis* 12, no. 2 (April 1980): esp. pp. 150–151.

10. Michael P. Todaro, "Urbanization in developing nations: Trends, prospects and policies," *Journal of Geography* 79, no. 5 (September/October 1980): 164–174.

11. The number of people in the developing world grew by about 72 percent between 1950 and 1975, from approximately 1.6 to 2.8 billion (*Patterns of Urban and Rural Population Growth,* cited in note 8, pp. 11 and 14).

12. Michael P. Todaro, *Economic Development in the Third World* (New York: Longman, 1977), p. 148.

13. International Bank for Reconstruction and Development, *Rural Development,* Sector Policy Paper (Washington, D.C.: February 1975), p. 4.

14. G. R. Saini, *Farm Size, Resources, Use Efficiency and Income Distribution (A Study in Indian Agriculture with Special Reference to Uttar Pradesh and Punjab)* (Bombay: Allied LMTD, 1979), p. 154. Under extreme circumstances in various parts of the developing world, wealthier farmers or moneylenders were able to buy out small farmers who came upon hard times or could no longer maintain their uneconomical plots.

15. I. Little, Tibor Scitovsky, and Maurice Scott, *Industry and Trade in Some Developing Countries* (London: Oxford University Press, 1970), p. 42.

16. S. R. Lewis, "Agricultural taxation and intersectoral resource transfers," Discussion Paper 134, Institute for Development Studies, Nairobi, 1971.

17. *Rural Development,* cited in note 13, pp. 83–84.

18. Raisuddin Ahmed, "Foodgrain supply, distribution and consumption policies within a dual pricing mechanism: A case study of Bangladesh," Research Report no. 8 (Washington, D.C.: International Food Policy Research Institute, May 1979), p. 12.

19. *Patterns of Urban and Rural Population Growth*, cited in note 8, p. 17.

20. *Patterns of Urban and Rural Population Growth*, cited in note 8, p. 62.

21. There came to the United States alone some 1.2 million Irish and 0.9 million Germans between 1847 and 1855, slightly more than 1 million Germans and over 0.4 million Scandinavians between 1880 and 1885, and 1.8 million Italians between 1898 and 1907 (Brinley Thomas, *Migration and Economic Growth* [Cambridge: Cambridge University Press, 1954], p. viii).

22. George Beier, Anthony Churchill, Michael Cohen, and Bertrand Renaud, "The task ahead for the cities of the developing countries," *World Development* 4, no. 5 (1979): 389.

23. Todaro, cited in note 12, p. 172.

24. David Turnham and Ian Jaeger, *The Employment Problems in Less Developed Countries* (Paris: Organization for Economic Cooperation and Development, 1970).

25. *Patterns of Urban and Rural Population Growth*, cited in note 8, pp. 5–15. A comprehensive discussion of the informal sector can be found in Dipak Mazumdar, "The urban informal sector," *World Development* 6, no. 9/10 (September/October 1978); and W. Sinclair, *Urbanization and Labor Markets in Developing Countries* (New York: St. Martin's, 1978).

26. *Patterns of Urban and Rural Population Growth*, cited in note 8, pp. 18 and 46.

27. *Patterns of Urban and Rural Population Growth*, cited in note 8, p. 19.

28. *Patterns of Urban and Rural Population Growth*, cited in note 8, p. 41.

29. Beier et al., cited in note 22, p. 376.

30. R. N. Barret, "The Brazilian foreign exchange auction system: Regional and sectoral protective effects," unpublished Ph.D. dissertation, University of Wisconsin, 1972; and O. E. Reboucas, "Interregional effects of economic policies: Multi-sector general equilibrium estimates for Brazil," unpublished Ph.D. dissertation, Harvard University, 1974.

31. Irving Hoch, "Urban scale and environmental quality," in *Resources and Environmental Implications of U.S. Popu-*

lation Growth, ed. Ronald G. Ridker (Baltimore: Johns Hopkins University Press, 1973).

32. Glenn Firebaugh, "Structural determinants of urbanization in Asia and Latin America, 1950–1970," *American Sociological Review* 44 (April 1979): 200–201.

33. Barbara Ward, "A 'people' strategy of development," Communique no. 13 (Washington, D.C.: Overseas Development Council, 1973).

34. Lipton, cited in note 4, p. 247.

35. Celso Furtado, *Economic Development in Latin America* (Cambridge: Cambridge University Press, 1970), p. 56; Keith Griffin, *The Political Economy of Agrarian Change* (Cambridge: Harvard University Press, 1974); Saini, cited in note 14, p. 154; James P. Grant, "Growth from below: A people oriented development strategy," Development Paper no. 16 (Washington, D.C.: Overseas Development Council, December 1973), p. 11.

36. "Food needs of developing countries: Projections of production and consumption to 1990," International Food Policy Research Institute, Research Report no. 3, December 1977, p. 17.

37. A. K. Bhattacharyya, "Income inequality and fertility: A comparative view," *Population Studies* 29, no. 1 (1975): 5–19; Robert Repetto, "The interaction of fertility and the size distribution of income," Research Paper no. 8, Center for Population Studies, Harvard University, October 1974; Julian L. Simon, "Income, wealth and their distribution as policy tools in fertility control," in *Population and Development: The Search for Selective Interventions,* ed. R. Ridker (Baltimore: Johns Hopkins University Press, 1976), Chapter 2.

38. Sally Findley, *Planning Internal Migration: A Review of Issues and Policies in Developing Countries* (Washington, D.C.: United States Bureau of the Census, 1977), p. 94.

39. As reported in James C. Miller, *Regional Development: A Review of the State-of-the-Art* (Washington, D.C.: Agency for International Development, April 1979), p. 55.

40. Findley, cited in note 38, p. 86.

41. E. A. J. Johnson, *The Organization of Space in Developing Countries* (Cambridge: Harvard University Press, 1970), pp. 235–241.

42. Reported in Findley, cited in note 38, p. 83.

43. Dennis Anderson and Mark W. Leiserson, "Rural enterprise and nonfarm employment," World Bank Research Paper, January 1978, p. 19; Dennis Anderson and Mark W. Leiserson, "Rural nonfarm employment in developing countries," *Economic Development and Cultural Change* (January 1980): 230; *Patterns of Urban and Rural Population Growth,* cited in note 8, p. 70.

44. Reported in Enyinna Chuta and Carl Liedholm, "Rural non-farm employment: A review of the state of the art," Michigan State University, Rural Development Paper, no. 4, 1979, pp. 8–10. In many areas of Latin America, however, manufacturing is much more an urban activity. One reason may be that handicrafts have continued to be an important manufacturing activity in the countryside of Africa and Asia, whereas rural enterprises in Latin America were not able to compete against a more technologically advanced industry in urban centers.

45. Chuta and Liedholm, cited in note 44, p. 81.

46. Chuta and Liedholm, cited in note 44, p. 82.

47. *Rural Development,* cited in note 13, p. 7.

48. Reported in Findley, cited in note 38, p. 94.

49. Chuta and Liedholm, cited in note 44, p. 54.

50. Chuta and Liedholm, cited in note 44, p. 56.

51. Beier et al., cited in note 22, p. 388.

52. "Food needs of developing countries," cited in note 36, p. 22.

53. As reported in Erik Eckholm, "The dispossessed of the earth: Land reform and sustainable development," Worldwatch Paper, no. 30, June 1979.

54. Edgar Owens and Robert Shaw, *Development Reconsidered: Bridging the Gap Between Government and People* (Lexington, Mass.: Lexington Books, 1972), pp. 56–57.

55. *Rural Development,* cited in note 13, pp. 8–9.

56. Among these countries are Bolivia, Ecuador, Colombia, Mexico, Paraguay, Uganda, Peru, Chile, Brazil, Ethiopia, Taiwan, Bangladesh, Venezuela, Sri Lanka, the Philippines, Kenya, Thailand, Tanzania, El Salvador, and India (reported in Findley, cited in note 38, p. 81).

57. Reported in Findley, cited in note 38, p. 81.

58. Among these countries are Bolivia, Colombia, Ecuador, Ethiopia, Israel, Kenya, Malawi, Malaysia, Mexico, Nigeria, Paraguay, the Philippines, and Thailand (reported in Findley, cited in note 38, p. 84).

59. *Patterns of Urban and Rural Population Growth*, cited in note 8, p. 82; World Conference on Agrarian Reform and Rural Development, *Review and Analysis of Agrarian Reform and Rural Development in the Developing Countries Since the mid-Sixties* (Rome: Food and Agriculture Organization, 1979), p. 88.

60. *Patterns of Urban and Rural Population Growth*, cited in note 8, pp. 116 and 118.

61. Kathleen Cloud, "Sex roles in food production and food distribution systems in the Sahel," paper prepared for USAID Center for Educational Research and Development, Tucson, Arizona, 15 December 1977.

62. John McHale and Magda Cordell McHale, *Basic Human Needs* (New Brunswick, N.J.: Transaction Books, 1978), p. 38.

63. Todaro, cited in note 12, pp. 245–253. See also Ronald P. Dore, *The Diploma Disease: Education, Qualification, and Development* (Berkeley: University of California Press, 1976).

64. Reported in Findley, cited in note 38, p. 84.

65. Among these countries are Colombia, Bolivia, Mexico, Peru, Niger, Tanzania, Kenya, Senegal, Malaysia, Bangladesh, Taiwan, and Thailand (reported in Findley, cited in note 38, p. 85).

66. Reported in Findley, cited in note 38, p. 85.

67. Among these countries are Argentina, Brazil, Colombia, Chile, Ecuador, Guatemala, Honduras, India, Malaysia, Mali, Mexico, Nigeria, Pakistan, Peru, the Philippines, Thailand, and Venezuela (reported in Findley, cited in note 38, p. 95).

68. Reported in Findley, cited in note 38, p. 78.

69. International Bank for Reconstruction and Development, *World Development Report 1979* (Washington, D.C.: 1979), p. 78.

70. David Kochav, Halger Bohlen, Kathleen DiTullio, Ilman Roostal, and Nurit Wahl, *Financing the Development of*

Small Scale Industries (Washington, D.C.: IBRD, 1974), mimeo; "Rural enterprise and nonfarm employment," cited in note 43, pp. 45–46.

71. *World Development Report 1979*, cited in note 69, p. 76.

72. Chuta and Liedholm, cited in note 44, p. 76.

73. Reported in Chuta and Liedholm, cited in note 44, p. 74; "Rural enterprise and nonfarm employment," cited in note 43, p. 44.

74. Chuta and Liedholm, cited in note 44, pp. 75–76.

75. More on the subject can be found in Sara Jackson, *Economically Appropriate Technologies for Developing Countries: A Survey* (Washington, D.C.: Overseas Development Council, February 1972); Keith Marsden, "Progressive technologies for developing countries," *International Labour Review* 101, no. 5 (May 1970): 475–502; E. F. Schumacher, *Small is Beautiful: Economics as if People Mattered* (New York: Harper & Row, 1973).

76. "Rural enterprise and nonfarm employment," cited in note 43, p. 43.

77. Quoted from International Crops Research Institute for the Semi-arid Tropics, *1978 Annual Report*, Hyderabad, India, p. 237.

78. Saini, cited in note 14, pp. 149–150.

79. Quoted in Findley, cited in note 38, p. 82.

80. World Conference on Agrarian Reform and Rural Development, cited in note 59, p. 51.

81. Reported in Findley, cited in note 38, p. 82.

82. A broad study is the World Food and Nutrition Study, *The Potential Contributions of Research* (Washington, D.C.: National Academy of Sciences, 1977).

83. Lipton, cited in note 4, p. 264.

84. *International Food Policy Research Institute Report* 2, no. 1 (January 1980): 1.

85. Reported in Findley, cited in note 38, p. 90; Peter Peek and Guy Standing, "Rural–urban migration and government policies in low-income countries," *International Labour Review* 118, no. 6 (November–December 1979): 753–754.

86. Fran Gillespie, "Urbanization eluded, the ruralization of Paraguay between 1950 and 1972," St. Joseph's University, Philadelphia, 1979 (mimeo).

87. Gillespie, cited in note 86, p. 8.

88. Eckholm, cited in note 53, p. 7.

89. Eckholm, cited in note 53, p. 8.

90. John D. Montgomery, "Allocation of authority in land reform programs: A comparative study of administration processes and outputs," Research and Training Network, Agricultural Development Council, New York, March 1974; Solon Barraclough, *Agrarian Structure in Latin America* (Lexington, Mass.: D. C. Heath, 1973); Keith Griffin, "Policy options for rural development," *Oxford Bulletin of Economics and Statistics* 35, no. 4 (November 1973): 246–249.

91. Eckholm, cited in note 53, p. 33.

92. Lipton, cited in note 4, p. 331.

93. Eckholm, cited in note 53, p. 11.

94. Eckholm, cited in note 53, pp. 37–38.

95. Carl Eicher, Thomas Zalla, James Kocher, and Fred Winch, "Employment generation in African agriculture," Institute of International Agriculture Research Report no. 9, Michigan State University, July 1970, p. 28.

96. Lipton, cited in note 4, p. 333.

97. Hollis Chenery et al., *Redistribution with Growth* (London: Oxford University Press, 1974).

98. Irma Adelman and Cynthia Taft Morris, *Economic Growth and Social Equity in Developing Countries* (Palo Alto: Stanford University Press, 1973), p. 186; Lipton, cited in note 4, p. 167; David Morawetz, *Twenty-five Years of Economic Development, 1950 to 1975* (Washington, D.C.: IBRD, 1977), p. 71.

99. *World Development Report 1980*, cited in note 1, Chapter 2.

MICHAEL P. TODARO is Senior Associate at the Center for Policy Studies of the Population Council and Professor of Economics at New York University. Previously he was Deputy Director of the Center for Policy Studies, Associate Director of Social Sciences at the Rockefeller Foundation, and Visiting Senior Lecturer at the University of Nairobi. Dr. Todaro received his Ph.D. from Yale University. He has traveled and lectured widely throughout Asia and Latin America, and has spent over five years of teaching and research in Africa. In addition to numerous articles in professional journals focused on issues of urbanization and rural-urban migration, he wrote *Development Planning: Models and Methods, Economic Theory, Internal Migration in Developing Countries*, and two leading textbooks, widely used in the United States and overseas, *Economic Development in the Third World* and *Economics for a Developing World*.

JERRY STILKIND is a Washington-based freelance writer. He has worked with the Twentieth Century Fund, as a congressional aide to a member of the House Foreign Affairs Committee, and as a reporter for various nationally known newspapers.

a Public Issues paper of
The Population Council

80-12
Printed in the U.S.A

PI-04
ISBN 0-87834-042-4